Country
Woodworker

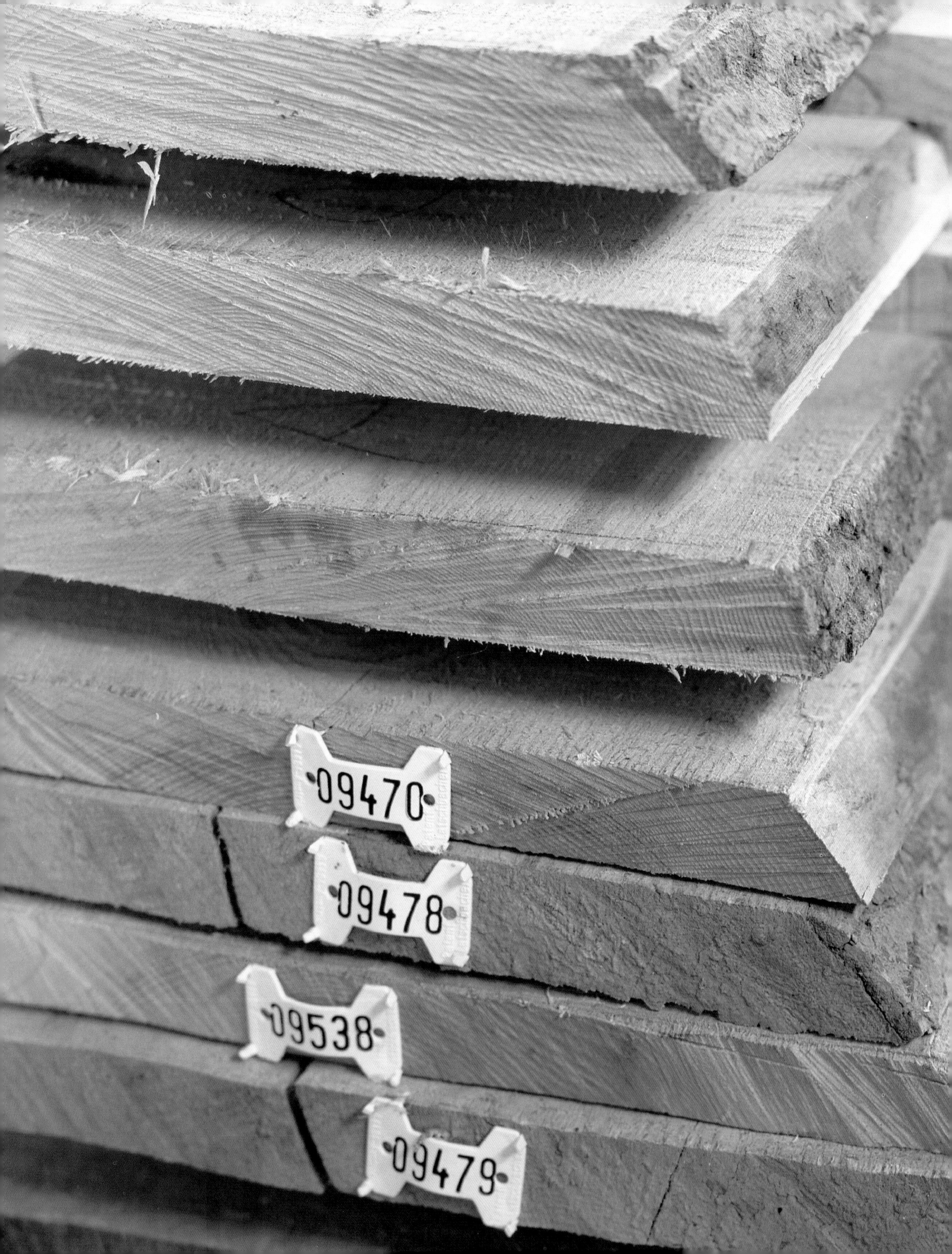
09470
09478
09538
09479

Country Woodworker

HOW TO MAKE

RUSTIC FURNITURE, UTENSILS,

AND DECORATIONS

JACK HILL

PHOTOGRAPHY BY JAMES MERRELL

CHRONICLE BOOKS
SAN FRANCISCO

Printed in China.
Cover design by Sharon Smith.

Library of Congress Cataloging-in-Publication Data:

Hill, Jack, 1933–
    Country woodworker: how to make rustic furniture, utensils, and
decorations / by Jack Hill.
    160 p.   24.2 x 29.3 cm.
    Includes index.
    ISBN 0-8118-1086-0 HC   0-8118-1589-7 PB
    1. Rustic woodwork. 2. Furniture making. 3. House furnishings;
I. Title.
    TT200.H48   1995
    684'.08—dc20   94-44479
                                           CIP

Distributed in Canada by Raincoast Books
8680 Cambie Street
Vancouver, B.C. V6P 6M9

10 9 8 7 6 5 4 3 2 1

Chronicle Books
85 Second Street
San Francisco, CA 94105

CONTENTS

INTRODUCTION:

LIVING WITH WOOD   8

LIVING ROOMS   14

Candle Box   22

Milking Stool   26

Decoy Duck   30

Candle Stand   34

Side Table   38

WOOD OUTSIDE	44	BEDROOMS & BATHROOMS	104
Bird House	50	Shaker Shelves & Pegboard	116
Five-Board Bench	54	Hooded Cradle	120
Traditional Whirligig	58	Blanket Box	124
Rocking Chair	64	Folk Bed	128
Rustic Chair	68		
		TOOLS & TECHNIQUES	132
KITCHENS & DINING ROOMS	72	WOOD GUIDE	148
Spoon Rack & Spoons	86	TEMPLATE PATTERNS	150
Scoops & Ladles	90	DIRECTORY OF SUPPLIERS	156
Cutting Boards	94	INDEX	158
Wall-Hung Cupboard	98	ACKNOWLEDGMENTS	160

Living with Wood

Wood is the most used of all our natural resources. Like food, wood has sustained humanity's basic needs since earliest times. Early cultures are dated by the materials used in ax-making – the Stone, Bronze, and Iron Ages – tools developed for cutting wood and for using as weapons of war. Together, wood and the ax provided early mankind with fuel for fire and, later, with shelter, too.

EVOLVING SKILLS AND TECHNIQUES

Throughout the ancient world, in Egypt, across Asia, and in Europe and the Americas, wood was used for buildings, furniture making, and a host of household wares and agricultural implements. Workers in wood came to recognize the different properties of various trees and so developed techniques for using them more advantageously. Medieval artisans learned how to cut, shape, carve, and, above all, how to make joints. Although their early efforts produced simple joints, they were solidly made – so much so that some examples have lasted until the present day. Throughout this period, new tools and working methods were evolving, and in due course, furniture and artefacts made by craftsmen in the cities eventually reached a high level of sophistication.

In the countryside, however, village woodworkers – often using the simple ax, adze, and auger – continued to make pieces of furniture in a plainer style. These pieces catered to the requirements of a rural people more interested in function than in fashion. The trees that provided the raw material for these enterprises were in abundant supply locally, and as more of the world was explored by the European seafaring nations, trees – both familiar species as well as new ones – were found to be widespread and even more plentiful. And since trees grow and can thus be cultivated, it was eventually recognized that trees could potentially provide a constant supply of useful material, and so become a renewable resource – a fact that is still not universally appreciated even today.

Experience soon showed that the wood from one tree was better than that from another for certain applications. Ash, for example, is very strong yet elastic, well able to withstand hard shocks, and so it was used extensively in making handles for tools. Oak – once a plentiful source of wood – is both strong and hard and its heart wood is extremely durable. It is also quite heavy. It was used widely in building work and furniture making.

THE COLONIAL ERA

When exploration gave way to colonization, the early settlers in the New World found trees with similar characteristics and properties to those that grew in their native lands: they discovered new ones, too, some with very different properties. Trees were everywhere, and they first had to be felled to make way for settlements and to provide cleared land for crops. The process of clearing the land for cultivation produced masses of wood for building and firewood. Once more, basic needs of food, shelter, and fuel were to be satisfied, and the most useful tool proved yet again to be the ax.

There is no doubt that the thought uppermost in the minds of those early colonists was simple survival. What they did first was what was needed most, and when it came to furniture making, the same priorities applied. A table, stools, bed, and perhaps a chair or cradle, a chest or cupboard for storage, and a few kitchen utensils – little else was actually needed.

Left - ALL THE INGREDIENTS OF THE COUNTRY STYLE ARE BROUGHT TOGETHER HERE – LIMEWASHED, BARE STONE WALLS, PLAIN FLOORBOARDS, AND EXPOSED WOODEN BEAMS. THE TABLE AND CHAIRS ARE INSPIRED BY THE WORK OF THE SHAKERS. DRYING HERBS AND HANGING BASKETS COMPLETE THE LOOK.

Above - THIS STURDY "STABLE DOOR" WITH ITS WROUGHT IRON ATTACHMENTS IS A FITTING EXAMPLE OF THE COLLABORATIVE WORK OF WOODWORKER AND BLACKSMITH. ORIGINAL DOORS SUCH AS THIS ARE NOW QUITE RARE DUE TO THE RAVAGES OF "RESTORERS" AND THE FASHION FOR REPLACING OLD WITH NEW.

A RETURN TO BASICS

Although there was wood to be found in abundance, there were few tools with which to work it. As a result, the first utensils and pieces of furniture were very plain and severely functional. Those who made it, familiar as they might well have been with the more sophisticated styles of contemporary European tastes, were by the nature of their circumstances obliged to adopt the more simple, rural tradition of working wood – a style typical of an English, Dutch, or Scandinavian village carpenter. In spite of evidence that there were skilled craftsmen among the early settlers, they returned purposefully to the work and working methods of the country woodworker, using their ingenuity and skills to make the best of what they had and what they knew.

These pioneer woodworkers used solid-wood construction, and because nails and screws were difficult to obtain and glue virtually unheard of, they used dovetail and housing joints and pegged or wedged their mortise and tenons, just as their European counterparts had done for thousands of years.

Inevitably, colonists from the different countries that settled in the Americas brought with them their own traditions, which were to have an impact on local furniture making, as did the contribution of some religious communities, such as the Shakers and the Amish. New England, Spanish and Dutch Colonial, Pennsylvania German, French, Scandinavian, are all representative of what we now call American "country" furniture. In Europe, the different countries retained their individual styles, and even within countries regional variations existed and exist still. The wide range of styles in painted furniture to be found in the European continent is a good example of this rich diversity.

AN APPRECIATION OF COUNTRY STYLE

Today, what was made in the village workshops of 18th- and 19th-century Europe and in the backwoods and early settlements of colonial America, is highly regarded on account of its simple beauty and stark utility. It has come to epitomize a particular time and way of life, a time when things were more natural and the pace more relaxed than it is today in our technology-driven world. Country woodwork, perhaps more than anything else, is central to the so-called country style; the very essence of country living.

Yet "country" is more than just a style, much more than simply a fashion or a fad. Rather, it is of enduring interest, a rich treasury of ideas and images, a heritage of past practices and traditions, something timeless in its simplicity. It was a style born out of necessity to people grateful merely to survive, unpretentious yet independently creative. In their self-sufficiency and in their adaptability, these craftsmen relied solely on traditional skills, limited tools, and the availability of natural resources.

The two-fold purpose of this book is to show you how the furniture and wooden artefacts of these bygone ages can contribute toward a country style of living, and, in a very practical way, to provide the means of achieving this objective. The inspirational pages that open each new section are packed with exciting design ideas for creating a whole country look; the practical projects that follow encourage you to make your own hand-crafted pieces, which, in time, may become heirlooms in their own right, cherished by later generations. Living with wood is undeniably pleasurable and working with wood can be deeply satisfying and rewarding. Here, within these pages, is all you need to know to become a country woodworker.

Above - SUNSHINE SHINING THROUGH A WOVEN SCREEN DAPPLES THE SEAT OF THIS RATHER UNUSUAL CHAIR. IT IS A FAIRLY MODERN PIECE, AND ITS DESIGN IS BASED ON A STYLE FOUND IN PARTS OF RURAL IRELAND, WHERE IT IS USUALLY KNOWN AS A SLIGO CHAIR.

Right - THE CORNER OF THIS COUNTRY KITCHEN SHOWS A MIXTURE OF OLD AND NEW. THE MODERN KITCHEN STOVETOP TO THE LEFT OF THE DOOR IS FLANKED BY A SIMPLE CUPBOARD LADEN WITH COLORFUL CONTAINERS AND WOODEN BOWLS DATING FROM THE 19TH CENTURY.

Living Rooms

There is a clear line of descent from the original rural cottage, where families once lived, ate, and sometimes slept crowded together in a single room, to today's modern country living room. Generations ago, the one-room rural cottage and its hearth was the center of all domestic activity and, no less today, the living room remains a focal point and gathering place for family and friends. Where once its furnishings and decoration were determined by basic necessities, the essential ingredients of the living room now are comfort and relaxation. With perhaps the exception of the kitchen (see pages 72-85), it provides the least private, yet the most homey, room in the house. It is, in the strictly literal sense, a room for living in.

EARLIER TIMES REMEMBERED

The average rural family room of earlier times was a simple affair, and even by the 19th century most families who lived off the land made do with the barest minimum of furniture and enjoyed few creature comforts. But wherever a cottager or small farmer was a little more prosperous, there was a discernible element of coziness. Here is how the English social historian and novelist Flora Thompson describes cottages in the 1880s: "In nearly all the cottages there was but one room downstairs, and many of these were poor and bare, with only a table and a few chairs and stools for furniture and a superannuated potato-sack thrown down by way of a hearthrug. Other rooms [in other cottages] were bright and cosy with dressers of crockery, cushioned chairs, pictures on the wall and brightly colored hand-made rag rugs on the floor. In these there would be pots of geraniums, fuchsias and old-fashioned, sweet smelling musk on the window sills. In the older cottages there were grandfather clocks, gate legged tables and rows of pewter . . ." (*Lark Rise to Candleford*, 1945.)

THE ELEMENTS OF COUNTRY STYLE

It is the descriptive atmosphere of rural coziness from the likes of Flora Thompson that should be your guide in creating a true country style in today's family living room. Starting with the basics, paint walls, whether plastered or wood-boarded, in country colors such as cream, soft blues, greens, or pinks. Plastered walls can also be wallpapered – for patterns, choose simple stripes or miniprints with naturalistic motifs such as acorn and leaf. Soft furnishings should also reinforce the country theme. Fabrics for curtains can be plain, striped, checked or, for prettiness, a traditional chintz. Combine them with checks and stripes in natural fabrics such as cotton and linen, and linen blends for chair and settee covers. Woven blankets and hand-made quilts complement the rugged texture of wood and add both color and comfort. Use them as throws over armchairs and settees or as wallhangings.

When it comes to the furniture, nothing should be too perfect, too precious, or too highly polished. No matching sets of chairs and no built-in furniture. For this is not the equivalent of the "drawing room" of more opulent households or the descendant of the 19th-century parlor. Furniture should be functional without being too formal, durable without being too utilitarian. And wood – with its textural surface quality and hand-worked mellow tones in perfect harmony with the simple, homey ambience – is, of course, the ideal material to create this mood and purpose.

The room itself needs to be carefully studied, since it may have much to contribute to the desired atmosphere. Wood is often the feature of wall construction, either as part or all of its structure, or it can be applied as paneling. Exposed wooden beams, kept natural and not painted, are in many instances central to the country cottage look.

Above - FROM THE HEAVY CEILING BEAMS TO THE LIGHTWEIGHT LADDERBACK CHAIRS, THE VERSATILITY OF WOOD IN A RURAL SETTING IS CLEARLY DEMONSTRATED. THE PINE TABLE AND THE CHAIRS ARE FROM THE SHENANDOAH VALLEY IN VIRGINIA, THE SOFA IS IN THE COUNTRY CHIPPENDALE STYLE.

Right - THE FIREPLACE IS OFTEN THE FOCUS OF A ROOM, AND PARTICULARLY SO IN A LIVING ROOM WHERE, AS HERE, THE MOST COMFORTABLE SEATING NATURALLY FINDS A PLACE AROUND IT. WOVEN AND QUILTED TEXTILES PROVIDE BRIGHT SPLASHES OF WARMTH AND COLOR.

Above - THE SIMPLE CONSTRUCTION OF THIS TWO-TIER HUTCH CUPBOARD IN PAINTED YELLOW PINE IS TYPICAL OF THE EARLY NEW ENGLAND STYLE. A WELL-MADE, UNPRETENTIOUS PIECE, IT LOOKS AT HOME IN ANY ROOM IN THE HOUSE.

Right - SETTLES WERE ORIGINALLY BUILT INTO THE FABRIC OF THE WALL, BUT BY THE END OF THE 16TH CENTURY, THEY WERE FREESTANDING AND HAD MOVED CLOSER TO THE HEARTH. THIS LOVELY SETTLE IS A FINE EXAMPLE OF AN EARLY 18TH-CENTURY "BACON SETTLE" – SO-CALLED BECAUSE THE CUPBOARD BUILT INTO THE FRAMED PANEL BACK PROVIDED SPACE IN WHICH TO HANG A SIDE OF BACON. THE SEAT LIFTS UP TO REVEAL A BOX FOR STORAGE.

Beams give a room character and strength. They speak for the structure of the whole building and of the work of nameless village carpenters or pioneer woodsmen of long ago, the marks left by their simple tools their only epitaph.

The focus of this family room is the fireplace – the hearth, once the main, or perhaps the only, source of warmth and light. The fireplace may be of the open "inglenook" variety, deep enough and high enough to walk into, topped with a massive, smoke-blackened beam of oak or elm. Or it may be smaller and a little lower, with a mantel shelf above for displaying ornaments and family memorabilia.

The hearth has always been a special place in the home, and it still is. An open fire, with brightly burning logs and the tangy smell of wood smoke, evokes primitive senses in us, and perhaps cherished memories, too, while its flickering light casts mysterious shadows and an elusive glow around the room, reflecting back from polished surfaces or people's faces. Where an open fire is impractical for some reason, consider using the space for an alternative source of heat, such as a traditional cast-iron woodburning stove or a natural gas-fired equivalent.

Around the fire are to be found the most comfortable chairs in the house. These are an invitation to sit and savor the delights of the time and place; a subtle suggestion that you have done enough for the day and now should pause and take time for yourself. For children, low stools will keep them close to the fire's glow; for adults, choose a sturdy Windsor – a comfortable design despite its rigidly wood appearance – or an upholstered chair, for both are at home by the hearth. Here, as elsewhere, the outdoor look of the Adirondack style of rustic furniture blends seamlessly into this informal setting. These pieces, made from wood that is rough-hewn and untreated, bring into the home the feel not just of the wood, but of the forest itself.

THE SEARCH FOR COMFORT

When the concept of comfort in the home came to be a subject of serious consideration sometime in the 16th century, it was usually related to the source of heat in a room. That, and the avoidance of drafts. Central-heating systems, insulation, and draft-proofing tend to solve the problem today, but in earlier times it was the furniture makers who provided at least the partial answer in the form of the high-backed settle.

Illustrations of comfortable 17th-century inns and cozy cottage interiors frequently depict deep, warm fireplaces flanked by a settle or, more often, a pair of settles, one on each side. When settles are used in this fashion, an enclosed space is formed, separate from the rest of the room, combining fireside seating for several people with adequate protection from the ever-present menace of drafts.

A true country piece of furniture, the settle was never accepted into the fashionable drawing rooms of the affluent – not, that is, until it had altered its shape and acquired an upholstered form, to be reborn as the settee, sofa, or couch. It is said that the settle is a development of the chest, which had always invited use as a seat, along with its other function as a boxlike storage container. Adding a back and arms to a chest easily produces the box settle, which is the proper name given to those pieces that incorporate a lidded storage space below the seat. An added refinement came in the form of draft-excluding end pieces – shaped head-protection pieces later adopted in the design of the still-popular wing armchair.

ADAPTING A BASIC DESIGN

Resourceful woodworkers have adapted the settle, more than any other piece of furniture, to a number of ingenious, multipurpose functions. By having a back that folded over on hinges, it was made to be converted into a useful table. This design was popular both in Europe and in colonial America, where it was usually made of pine. The usual modern name for this type of converting settle-table is monks' bench, a name that is probably erroneous, since these pieces are more closely associated with wayside inns than with monasteries.

In some places, especially where space was limited, the settle-bed was popular. Acting as a long seat by day, its bottom portion could be opened out at night to provide a comfortable box bed. When they were not in use for sleeping purposes, the mattress and bed clothes could be conveniently stored inside out of the way. Parallels with the modern convertible sofabed are obvious. One other use of the settle – one that has, fortunately, not carried over to the present day – was the use of the lower part as a coop to house a laying hen or goose.

Many high-backed settles, like the one shown below, had cupboards in the back in which sides of bacon were hung, presumably to cure. Such cupboards – and others, both wall-hung and floor-standing and used for food storage – were once very common and are the ancestors of many, much grander, cabinets and cupboards used for a wide variety of different purposes today.

The name cupboard derives from the medieval "cup-borde," literally a board for storing cups or drinking vessels, often arranged in tiers with one board above another, in a fashion similar to what we now simply call shelves. In the Middle Ages, a closer equivalent to the modern cupboard was the English "aumbry" or the French

"armoire." These were simple boxlike structures, but were, significantly, fitted with a door. Their main use seems to have been for storing food and other goods. Today, cupboards and cabinets of all types serve a variety of useful functions and feature in the living room, and elsewhere, for many varied general-storage purposes.

A cupboard in a country-style living room is an ideal candidate for a variety of decorative paint treatments, including stenciling, woodgraining, and distressing. In the past, cupboards and many other wooden items of furniture in cottages and country houses were painted with milk paint (see page 146 for details) in a range of earth colors such as cream, buff, gray green, duck-egg blue, brick red, and ox-blood red. Milk paint was widely used by the early settlers in North America, as the ingredients – buttermilk or skimmed milk, pigment, and a little lime – were readily available and the results were attractive and long-lasting. With age, milk paint takes on an attractive, mellow patina. The effect of wear and tear on a newly painted piece can easily be re-created by gently rubbing the paint here and there with sandpaper or steel wool to reveal the wood beneath.

Left & Above - THE LIVING ROOM OF THIS MASSACHUSETTS HOME IS PART OF A PAIR OF RESTORED BARNS. THE FURNITURE HAS BEEN CHOSEN TO COMPLEMENT THE HIGH CEILINGS AND RUGGED BEAMS, AND INCLUDES A STURDY PINE CUPBOARD AND A SIMPLE HANGING CUPBOARD, BOTH PAINTED AND DISTRESSED.

- C A N D L E -
B O X

Small boxes of all types were once a common feature in country households. They were used to hold all manner of things, from salt and spices to knives, spoons and, of course, candles, or whatever needed to be put away safely where it could be readily found. The earliest examples were wall boxes. These were made either to hang from a peg or nail on the wall or designed to sit up against a wall supported on a table or ledge. In their simplest form, these boxes were lidless. Others, however, did have lids, and as the design developed, further elaboration in the form of drawers took place until the box was sometimes transformed into a miniature set of drawers. This evolution is analogous to that of the chest (see page 124).

Boxes have been given names according to their main use, and in addition to those mentioned above, there are, among others, bobbin boxes for storing lacemaking bobbins, dice and domino boxes, and pipe boxes. English country inns once had tobacco boxes, the locked lids of which were opened by pushing a coin through a slot. This allowed the smoker to fill his pipe and pay for it on trust:

> *The custom is, before you fill,*
> *To put a penny in the till;*
> *When you have filled, without delay,*
> *Close the lid or sixpence pay.*

Some boxes had no specific use, but were merely for keeping important documents, letters, simple personal treasures, or a valuable book safe. These, appropriately, were known as keeping boxes. Quite often, such boxes were intricately decorated by their owners on the outside with paintings or carvings to attest to the value placed on them and their contents.

While it may be difficult for us today, with our built-in cupboards and kitchen cabinets, to appreciate fully just how invaluable boxes were in the past, they still can serve a useful purpose over and above a decorative one. The candle box featured here makes an ideal letter rack or a place to keep household accounts, while other boxes can be modified to suit all types of modern application.

Right - BELOW THE MANTEL SHELF OF THIS LARGE OPEN HEARTH, TO THE LEFT, HANGS A SMALL WALL BOX IN THE SAME DESIGN AS THAT GIVEN IN THE PROJECT THAT FOLLOWS. HERE IT SERVES AS A USEFUL STORAGE PLACE FOR CANDLES READY FOR USE, OR POSSIBLY FOR TAPERS TO LIGHT THE FIRE.

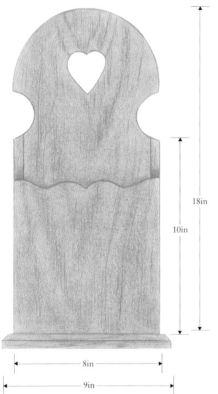
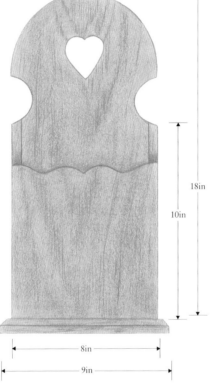

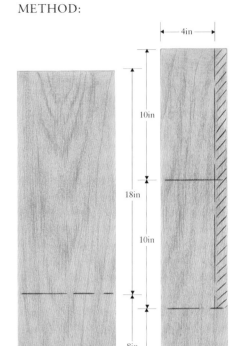

ABILITY LEVEL: Novice/Intermediate

SIZE: 18 x 9 x 6½ inches

MATERIALS: Pine, Cherry, Oak

CUTTING LIST:
1 back
18 x 8 x ½ inches

1 front
8 x 8 x ½ inches

2 sides
10 x 5 x ½ inches

1 bottom
9 x 6½ x ½ inches

See template patterns on page 152 for shaped and cut-out pieces.

All measurements are given in inches.

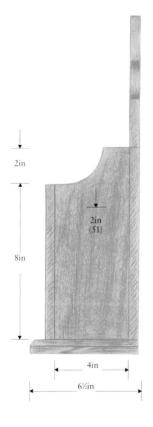

METHOD:

1. Mark and cut out the separate pieces to size. They can be cut economically from two pieces of wood as shown. Mark each piece for its intended use.

2. Trace the full-sized template patterns on page 152 and transfer the shapes to the appropriate pieces of wood.

3. Cut the pieces to shape.

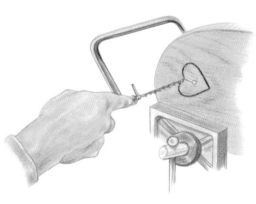

4. For the internal heart shape, first drill through the wood and then enlarge the hole with a scroll saw or coping saw. Finish off with a file and sandpaper.

5. Clean off all tool marks on the sawn edges. Check that everything is cut to size and that the side pieces are a matching pair.

6. Assemble the back, front, and side pieces without using glue. Check the alignment of matching edges of the shaped pieces. Make any necessary adjustments.

7. Mark and cut out a ¼-inch chamfer on the front and side top edges of the bottom base-piece.

8. Clean up all the component pieces ready for assembly.

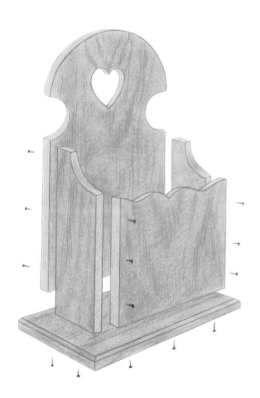

9. Glue and nail all the box components together as shown. Use small brads or finishing nails and take extra care not to split the wood when you are nailing, especially if you have used a hardwood to make the box (see page 141 for advice on nailing).

10. Begin by fixing the back to the sides, then add the front. Check that everything is square before attaching the bottom in place. Remove any surplus glue and leave to dry thoroughly.

11. Set nail heads below the surface and fill the indentations with wood putty or with a mixture of glue and sawdust.

12. Apply a suitable indoor finish. A traditional beeswax polish will give a warm glow to the wood, especially after a number of applications; varnish will give a tougher, more protective finish. If you want to give your box a well-aged appearance, try one of the special techniques such as distressing the wood, applying an "antique" wood stain, or painting the box and then distressing the paintwork (see pages 146-7 for details).

13. The box can be hung on a wall using two nails, hooks, or small pegs through the heart-shaped cutout, or you can use a standard mirror plate that screws onto the back of the box. The box can also be freestanding and be placed on a table or perhaps on a window ledge.

Above - THIS FINE COLLECTION OF KITCHEN ARTE-FACTS INCLUDES A CANDLE BOX AND A WOODEN SCOOP WITH A DECORATIVE CHIP-CARVED HANDLE (ONLY PARTLY SHOWN.)

Left - THIS CANDLE BOX WAS MADE BY FOLLOWING THESE INSTRUCTIONS. TO COMPLETE THE LOOK, IT WAS TREATED WITH A CLEAR ANTIQUE FINISH.

MILKING STOOL

Before the notion of intensive farming became a reality, and the introduction of milking machines a necessity, individual cows in old-style dairies were milked by hand. For centuries, ever since the domestication of the cow, there had been no other way, and indeed, mechanical milking became possible only when an automated mechanism that imitated the quite complex movements of the human hand was perfected.

While milking by hand, the farm lad or dairy maid would sit on a low, sturdy stool, usually constructed with three legs in a tripod arrangement. Even if they were never used for this specific purpose, such three-legged stools are today collectively known as milking stools. The splayed arrangement of legs was a necessary functional design, for it provided stability on the often uneven stone or dry earth floors that were typical of early farm buildings. And for milking purposes, the tripod of legs served another important need – they allowed the sitter to lean forward on two legs, "into" the cow, without losing balance.

The majority of milking stools have circular seats or tops, although some have a straight front edge with a pair of legs at each corner and a round back edge with a central third leg. This design, too, can be easily tilted forward. Stools with square seats and four legs are more likely to have been for household use. Early designs had riven (cleft) legs, split from a log and roughly shaped by drawknifing, or were made from suitable branchwood. Legs were commonly joined to the tops by means of through joints secured by wedging. It is possible that, in the absence of a boring tool, leg holes would have been burned through the seat with a red-hot iron bar.

Even if you don't keep a cow around the house, as was very commonplace in country regions throughout Europe and North America until relatively recent times, a milking stool will still make a positive contribution to a country-style living room fireside or a rustic looking kitchen. Children also love them because they don't stand too high off the ground. But a word of caution is needed here: don't allow anybody to stand on them; with only three legs, they can easily topple over if the weight is off-center.

Left - A LATE 18TH-CENTURY COUNTRY HOUSE IN VAKSALA, SWEDEN, PROVIDES THE IDEAL SETTING FOR A VARIETY OF AUTHENTIC SWEDISH RUSTIC FURNITURE. IN FRONT OF THE BLAZING FIRE SITS A 19TH-CENTURY PINE MILKING STOOL, WELL WORN FROM YEARS OF SERVICE.

ABILITY LEVEL: Novice/Intermediate

SIZE: 10 x 10 x 8 inches

MATERIALS:
(**Top**) Elm, Oak, Pine
(**Legs**) Ash, Beech, Maple, Oak

CUTTING LIST:
1 top
10 x 10 x 2 inches

3 legs
8 x 2 x 2 inches

All measurements are given in inches.

METHOD:

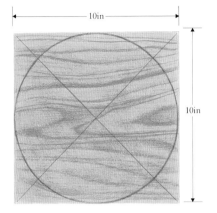

1. Using a compass, mark the top piece to a 10-inch diameter circle and cut to shape. This forms the template for the stool top.

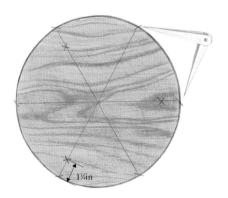

2. Choose the best surface to be the top and, with the compass still set to give a 5-inch radius, mark six equal points around the circumference of the top piece.

3. Join these six points with pencil lines and on these mark the three leg positions for drilling 1¼ inches in from the edge.

4. These three holes are drilled at a compound angle of 20° from the vertical. This can be done by eye, but only if you are very experienced. There are various techniques to help you to get this angle right. A simple way is to use a carpenter's sliding bevel set at 20° as a guide when drilling.

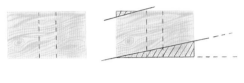

5. However, a more accurate method of working is to construct a predrilled guide block as shown here. When correctly made and clamped to the work, all you need to do is drill into the stool seat through the hole in the guide block.

6. Where a drill press is available, it is best to tilt the stool top and drill vertically into it. To do this, tilt the stool top up at the prescribed angle by raising one end on a block. Another, more secure, method is to make a tilting-table arrangement, as shown. Use a protractor to measure the angle of the table top, which is fixed by means of a supporting block. By aligning each pencil line on the stool top with a center reference line drawn on the tilting table, you should be able to angle holes consistently for the legs.

7. Drill three 1-inch diameter holes through the top. A saw-toothed bit is recommended (see page 139 for advice on drills).

8. Clean up the sawn edges of the top and bevel the edges for comfort.

9. Now turn your attention to the stool legs. These can be turned on a lathe, if one is available, using the dimensions given. However, stool legs were frequently shaped using a drawknife or spokeshave either to a roughly round section or an approximately hexagonal shape. A plane could also be used.

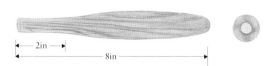

10. No matter which technique is used, the legs must be tapered at the top to carefully made, round tenon joints 1 inch in diameter and about 2 inches in length. This is best done with a spokeshave, but a rasp or file can be used.

11. Form each joint individually and try it frequently for size in the appropriate socket in the stool top. Bear in mind that although

the joint should be a good fit it does not have to be too tight at this stage, since it will be secured later by wedges.

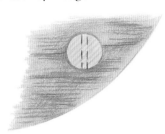

12. When all three legs fit, mark pencil lines on their ends to indicate the orientation of the saw cuts needed for the wedges. It is important that the wedges are inserted at right angles to the grain of the wood of the stool top. Otherwise, the force of the wedge could easily split the wood.

13. Remove the legs and make 1¼-inch saw cuts for the wedges.

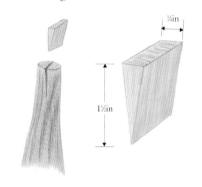

14. Following the dimensions given, make three wedges. Always use a hardwood for the wedges. Make sure that the grain runs down the length of the wedge and not across its width. Try using wood of a contrasting color to give the wedges an added decorative quality.

15. Clean up all the component pieces. Prepare to assemble the stool by first inserting a little glue into each leg socket. Next, fit the legs so that their tops protrude slightly through the top of the stool.

16. Align each leg so that the wedges will lie at right angles to the grain of the seat. (See step 12 above.)

17. Stand the stool upright on a flat, solid surface. Insert the wedges and tap each one partway in using a hammer. Then tap each

one again in turn until they fit tightly. The weight of a hammer is better for this than a wooden mallet.

18. Check the stability of the stool, wipe off any surplus glue, and leave it to dry.

19. When it is dry, saw off the protruding stub ends of the legs and wedges almost flush with the stool seat, taking care not to damage its surface. Clean off the saw marks with a sharp chisel or block plane.

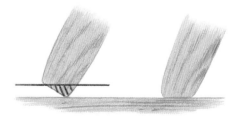

20. Mark and then saw or rasp off the inside bottom edges of each leg close to the angle made with the floor surface.

21. Smooth the completed stool with a fine-grade abrasive paper, if necessary.

22. Apply a suitable finish (see pages 146-7.) Traditionally, milking stools were left unfinished. Those used in the dairy were scrubbed clean using coarse sand.

More than a thousand years ago, Native Americans used dead and artificial birds as decoys to lure wild duck and other fowl within range of their weapons. These early artificial decoys were in the main quite crudely made, comprising bundles of aquatic rush either covered in real duck skins or simply painted and decorated with feathers. Other examples of decoys were nothing more than piles of mud and clay and bunches of dried grass tied onto sticks.

In Europe, a different method of wildfowling predominated. There, semidomesticated living birds were used to entice their unsuspecting brethren into specially made, tunnel-shaped capture nets. These lures were known as Coy Ducks, a name derived from the Dutch word *ende-kooy,* which means a duck cage or trap – and the original application of the word decoy.

When the first European settlers arrived in America, they found it expedient to adopt the local method – there were no domestic animals or birds readily at hand, and "living off the land" became a stark reality. In due course, however, dissatisfaction with the temporary and largely land-bound Indian decoy led to the introduction of a more permanent, floating decoy made from wood. Very simply made at first, and often blackened by charring in a fire or crudely painted, these early wooden decoys were more representational than realistic. However, properly ballasted and anchored

by stone weights on a string, they bobbed about in quite a lifelike manner, and even the crudest were generally successful in attracting unwitting live birds. Later, decoys became more sophisticated in construction and finish, and those from individual makers were extolled for their realism and their claimed effectiveness as lures.

The decoy method relies on the "instinct to forgather" of many species of wild water fowl, and other birds, too. For many, this trait resulted in extinction, or near extinction, as literally tens of thousands of birds fell each year, particularly during annual migratory flights, largely to "market gunners." These professional and expert marksmen shot to supply both a commercial market and an ever-increasing population. Such activity required a large number of decoys – a typical lone gunner might shoot over a "rig" of 40 to 50 decoys and bag hundreds of birds in a day. For a period, demand could be satisfied only by resorting to factory-made decoys, but these were never as attractive or as well made as the hand-made decoys.

Today, the law forbids duck shooting on this scale, although sports shooting is still permitted in season and under license. Decoys are still made and used along the shoreline and in the marshes, but many – particularly the old handmade ones – are now used only decoratively in the home, and the very best have become highly desirable and extremely collectible.

Left - A PARTICULARLY FINE COLLECTION OF LOCALLY MADE DECOYS BRIGHTENS UP THE MATTE EARTHY COLORS OF THIS NORTH AMERICAN COLONIAL HOME. THE ARMCHAIR, WHICH PROBABLY DATES FROM THE 17TH CENTURY, IS A NINE-SPINDLE DOUBLE-COMB BACK, A RARE NORTH AMERICAN WINDSOR VARIANT.

Above - DECOYS ARE MOST OFTEN OF THE FLOATING TYPE, BUT THE FORERUNNERS OF THESE, THE PROTOTYPE NORTH AMERICAN INDIAN DECOYS, WERE MADE PRIMARILY FOR USE ON LAND. LAND-BOUND DECOYS WERE KNOWN AS "STICK-UPS," OF WHICH THE ONE ABOVE IS A TYPICAL EXAMPLE.

ABILITY LEVEL: Intermediate

SIZE: 11 x 6 x 5 inches

MATERIALS: Pine

CUTTING LIST:
Body: 1 piece
11 x 5 x 3 inches

or Body: 2 pieces
11 x 2½ x 3 inches

Head
5½ x 2½ x 1½ inches

1 dowel
2 x ½ inches diameter

See template patterns on page 150 for the head and body.

All measurements are given in inches.

METHOD:

1. In making solid bodies, the early decoy maker would first cut the wood to length and then proceed to chop the block into the rough shape required using a sharp ax. Working at a chopping block of convenient height, he would first remove the corners, roughly round the breast, and shape the tail.

2. Next, with the roughly shaped body held in a vise, a drawknife or spokeshave was used to refine the shape. An area at the forward end was kept slightly oversize and flat to receive the head. In this process the maker used no patterns or templates, relying only on his skill and experience to achieve the required shape.

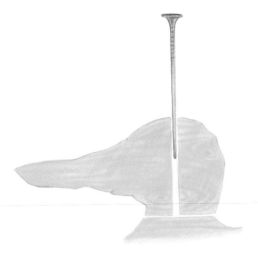

3. The head, which demands more careful attention, was sawn to profile, according to the species of bird, and then, with the wood held in a vise, it was bored to take a mounting dowel or nail.

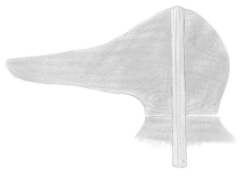

4. The shape of the assembled decoy was then finished off using a spokeshave or by whittling with a knife and finally sanded smooth before being painted.

5. To make a modern decoy, particularly one intended as an ornament, use the dimensions given and cut the body to size. If you are using two pieces of wood for the body, first glue them together and allow the glue to dry thoroughly before proceeding.

6. Using the template patterns given on page 150, begin the preliminary shaping using a saw. If you feel you have the necessary skill, an ax can be used for this.

7. Once you have the basic outline shape, start the detailed shaping using a drawknife or spokeshave, woodcarving tools, or knife. Reference to the cross-sections given with the templates will prove helpful in achieving the required shape (see page 150.) For safety, work with the wood in a vise or clamped to the bench during the shaping process.

8. Finish off the shaping with a file or knife, remembering to keep the forward area over-size and flat at this stage to accommodate the head.

9. Using the template on page 150, cut the head to shape using a bandsaw or coping saw. Make sure its base is square and flat.

10. Using a blind dowel is the best method of attaching the head to the body of a decorative decoy. For this, drill a ½-in hole down through the head and fit and glue a piece of dowel in place. As well as fixing the head, this dowel also provides a convenient grip for holding the wood while you finish off the final shaping.

11. Grip the base of the head piece in the vise and shape the main part of the head (using the template pattern and drawn details as a guide). Finish the detailing and the area around the base of the head, with the dowel already in place held in the vise. Take care not to crush the dowel.

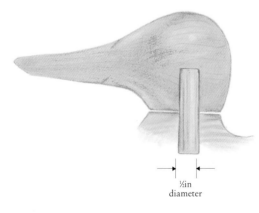

½in
diameter

12. Mark and drill the dowel hole in the body. Lightly plane the flat area left on the body to make a level jointing surface. Try the head for fit, without using glue, and adjust the mating surfaces if necessary until they fit comfortably. Then glue the head to the body and leave it to dry.

13. You can now finish any of the detailing of the decoy, filing and finally smoothing the surface ready for painting.

14. The paint finishes on early decoys were usually quite dull earth colors, and very little detailing, such as feathers or even eyes, was included. You can emulate this style and keep everything simple or try to produce a more realistic appearance. The shape of this decoy approximates that of a male mallard, and the model can be finished in appropriate plumage and colors. You could use a color photograph as a painting guide. See also page 146 for advice on painting.

Below - AGAINST THE LIGHT-WASHED BACKGROUND OF A PINE BOARDED WALL, A DECOY DUCK SITTING IN AN UNUSED SEED TRAY MAKES A PLEASING, THREE-DIMENSIONAL, STILL-LIFE PICTURE. A SEASONED PINE BENCH SITS COMFORTABLY BELOW IT.

CANDLE
STAND

There is evidence that candle making was establish as a trade in Europe as early as the 13th century. At first, candles would have been made with tallow – basically animal fat, which gives off a terrible stench when burned – but beeswax would also have been used. Although more expensive than tallow, beeswax has a far more agreeable aroma. However, it was the use of paraffin wax, first made in America by Abraham Gesner in 1846 and developed commercially by the Scotsman, James Young, that made candles less objectionable and more affordable, and ensured their popular and widespread use, even to the present day. Whenever soft lights and a romantic setting are called for, candles suit the occasion.

Candles are most often used in some form of candle holder, often a candlestick with a socket just large enough to accommodate the base of the candle. This would have been placed where the candle's limited throw of light could be used to best advantage. When extra height was needed, the candle stand was once a popular choice.

Candle stands are related to that group of furniture that includes pedestal and tripod tables; similarities in their design and construction are fairly obvious, and they differ mainly in terms of size and sophistication. An early reference is contained in an 11th-century manuscript now in the British Museum, which describes a small, round table on a central pillar above spreading feet. Candle stands probably reached their zenith of popularity in England shortly after the Restoration of Charles II in the 17th century, when highly ornate examples, along with equally ornate wall mirrors, became fashionable in the extravagant drawing rooms of the period.

However, the candle stand that features here is entirely utilitarian. It is simply made and solidly constructed, typical of the type used every day in Europe and in the early colonial period in North America. While some designs, including those of the Shakers, often incorporate a tripod arrangement of "feet" dovetailed into a lathe-turned column, this one features a more easily made – and stronger – cross-lapped-base construction. The square stem, which is chamfered into an octagonal shape, is secured to the base using a substantial dowel or mortise and tenon joint.

Right - THE CANDLE STAND CAN FULFIL A WIDE VARIETY OF FUNCTIONS IN THE MODERN HOME. HERE IT IS A HANDY DEPOSITORY FOR BOOKS, BUT IT COULD EQUALLY WELL SERVE AS A PEDESTAL FOR A FRESH OR DRIED FLOWER ARRANGEMENT OR AS A STAND FOR A PIECE OF SCULPTURE.

ABILITY LEVEL: Intermediate

SIZE: 27 x 13 x 13 inches

MATERIALS: Cherry, Oak

CUTTING LIST:
1 stem
24 x 2¼ x 2¼ inches

1 top
12 x 12 x 1 inches

1 brace
10 x 2 x 1 inches

2 feet
13½ x 2½ x 2 inches

1 dowel
3 x 1 inches diameter

All measurements are given in inches.

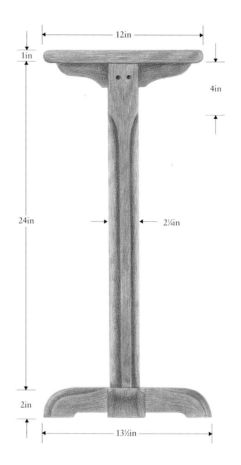

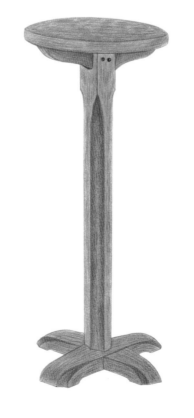

METHOD:

1. If you cannot obtain the top as one piece of wood, you will have to edge-join narrower pieces together (see page 141 for advice).

2. Make sure that the top is flat. If you have glued pieces together, wait until the glue is dry, and then plane the surfaces clean and smooth while the wood is still square (it is easier to hold at this stage).

3. Next, cut the top to a 12-inch diameter circle. Clean up the sawn edges and round over or chamfer them slightly, top and bottom.

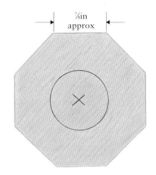

4. Cut the stem to length, making sure that both ends are square. Mark out the chamfers in pencil as a guide to planing. The finger gauging method on page 137 is accurate enough for this task.

5. Plane the four chamfers to produce the required octagonal shape. Allow the chamfers to taper off, leaving the top 4 inches square for the top lapped, or bridle, joint.

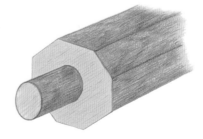

6. Make the bottom joint by drilling into the bottom of the stem and gluing in a piece of 1-inch diameter dowel. This peg joint will fit into a corresponding hole drilled into the assembled feet of the stand (see step 12). Drilled holes must be perfectly perpendicular to the stem.

7. As an alternative, this round joint can be worked in the solid on the end of the stem. Or a conventional, square mortise and tenon could be used instead (see page 144). In each case, add an extra 1½ inches to the stem length given.

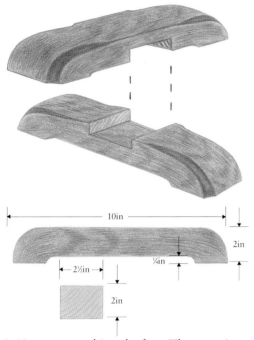

8. Now start making the feet. The two pieces are cross lapped or half lapped so that the top is flush where they cross over.

9. Mark out and cut each half of the joint as shown (see also page 143 for guidance). Check for a good, tight fit, make any adjustments that are necessary, and then take the joint apart.

10. Mark and cut out the scrolled shape of the two feet. Sand back the sawn surfaces and chamfer the top edges.

11. Reassemble the feet to make sure they fit and then glue the joint and clamp the wood together if necessary. Wipe off surplus glue and leave it to dry.

12. When it is dry, if using the dowel method, drill a 1-inch hole through the center of the cross lap. If a mortise and tenon is used, mark and cut out the mortise square through the center of the cross lap joint. Without gluing, check this joint for a good, tight fit with the stem dowel or tenon. Separate the pieces for the next stage.

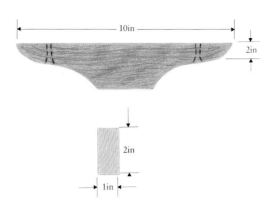

13. The brace that supports the top is lapped, full width, into the top of the stem, making what is also known as a bridle joint. Shape and then fit the brace to the underside of the top, as shown. It should lie across the grain of the top piece. Glue and screw it into position.

14. Mark and carefully cut out the housing for the brace on the top of the stem. Take your measurements from the brace itself since they may differ from those given. Check the joint for a good fit; it should not be too tight, since forcing it may split the stem.

15. Disassemble and clean up all the surfaces. When satisfied, glue the stem into the base feet. For extra security, the joint can be wedged (see page 29 for advice).

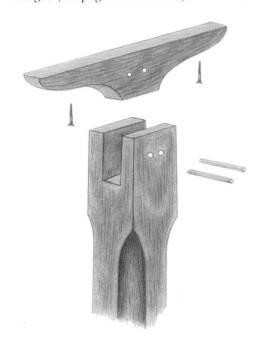

16. Next, glue the top into place by fitting the brace into its prepared housing. Secure

this by drilling two holes through the assembled joint and inserting ¼-inch dowel pegs, as shown. When the glue is dry, either cut these off flush or leave them slightly raised from the surface.

17. Remove any surplus glue and clean up all the surfaces.

18. In the past, the candle stand would either have been stained and polished or left its natural color and given a protective finish using beeswax. A wax finish will bring out the warm colors of the wood, and over time, and many applications, the color will become richer and deeper. You can achieve this effect more quickly by applying wood stain and then a coat of wax or perhaps a clear varnish (see pages 146-7 for advice on techniques for finishing).

SIDE
TABLE

Tables in medieval times were only temporary affairs – nothing more than a long board, or series of boards butted up together to make a wider surface, supported on wooden trestles. When the meal was finished, these trestle tables could easily be dismantled and removed. This type of furniture suited an era when communal living was commonplace and rooms were not specifically designated as having different functions as they are today. An interesting historical note is that "board" in this context is still used in such terms as "boarding house" and "board and lodgings." Over the years, board and trestle were joined together into a more permanent piece of furniture, which became known as the standing or "dormant" table. Chaucer, writing in the 14th century, refers to "his table dormant in his halle always." However, sometime early in the 16th century the design of tables changed significantly with the introduction of the frame construction, which gave rise to the "joyned" table.

Instead of a pair of trestles, the table now had four (or more) legs linked and braced by right-angled cross-rails at the top and stretcher rails at the bottom. Each part of this arrangement was mortised and tenoned together and carefully pegged for extra strength and stability. Many of these tables were of considerable size. But as both household requirements and architecture changed, so a need arose for different kinds of furniture, including smaller-sized tables. Initially, these were cut-down versions of the larger tables. Later they became lighter in construction and soon began to diversify markedly in style and construction, and include all kinds of clever contrivances to make smaller tables extendable into larger ones. Today there is a style of table suitable for virtually every room in the house and for all manner of specific occasions and uses.

One frequently seen design is the side table, sometimes known as an "occasional" table, an early 17th-century development. Square or rectangular, side tables were often made in pairs and were intended to stand at each end of the dining room. Some also came with semicircular tops.

The small side table shown here serves a number of potential functions. Its name gives it its proper position – it should be placed to one side against a wall where it might function as a writing table or as a small work table. Its large drawer is useful in both these roles. It would be equally at home in a kitchen. In the past, tables of this kind were generally made with a hardwood frame for strength and an inexpensive softwood top, such as pine. Everything would then be stained to match the frame. However, if the table was destined for the kitchen, the top would not be stained so that it could be kept clean by a scouring of water and gritty sand.

Left - A SIMPLY MADE SIDE TABLE SUCH AS THIS GIVES A REAL FLAVOR OF COUNTRY LIVING. IN MANY CASES, THE UNDERFRAME WOULD BE MADE FROM SOME TYPE OF HARDWOOD, TO GIVE STRENGTH TO THE CONSTRUCTION, WHILE THE TOP WOULD BE OF PINE FOR ECONOMY.

Above - RESPLENDENT WITH A CASUAL ARRANGEMENT OF FLOWERING WILD BROOM, THIS SIDE TABLE HAS AN OAK UNDERFRAME AND A TOP OF YELLOW PINE. A USEFUL DRAWER IS INCLUDED IN ITS CONSTRUCTION, WHICH IS DESCRIBED IN DETAIL IN THE PROJECT THAT FOLLOWS.

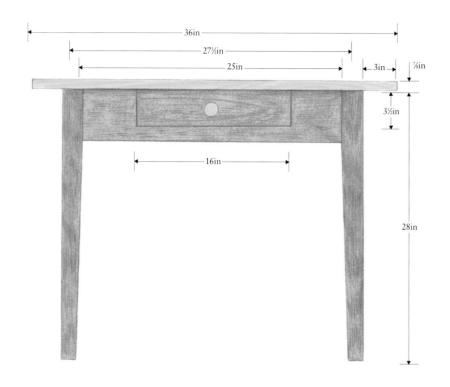

ABILITY LEVEL: Experienced

SIZE: 36 x 30 x 22 inches

MATERIALS:
(**Top**) Pine
(**Frame**) Oak, Cherry, Beech

CUTTING LIST:
1 top
36 x 22 x ⅞ inches

4 legs
28 x 2½ x 2½ inches

2 side rails
27½ x 5 x ⅞ inches

2 end rails
13½ x 5 x ⅞ inches

2 cross rails
14 x 2 x ⅞ inches

2 drawer runners
13 x ⅞ x ⅞ inches

1 drawer front
16 x 3½ x ⅞ inches

2 drawer sides
12 x 3½ x ½ inches

1 drawer back
16 x 3 x ½ inches

1 drawer bottom
13 x 16 x ¼ inches

All measurements are given in inches.

METHOD:

1. The top is made by edge-joining narrower boards. Begin by selecting straight pieces of pine, planing their mating edges, and joining them using the simple "rubbed joint" method, or an alternative method described on pages 141-2. If the top is to be left untreated for kitchen use, use a waterproof glue.

2. Glue up the top. Check that it is flat, apply glue to the mating edges and use a minimum of three clamps as shown and described on page 142.

3. Cut the frame materials to size. The legs are tapered and the frame is assembled with double mortise and tenon joints (see page 145 for advice on this joint).

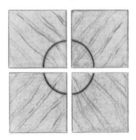

4. Mark the top ends of the legs with a pencil line as shown as a useful guide for all subsequent work.

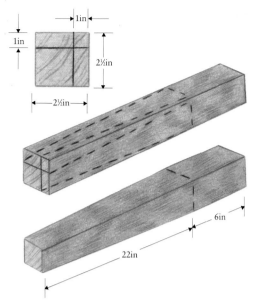

5. Taper the legs on two inside surfaces only, leaving the top 6 inches of the legs untapered. Remove the bulk of the waste wood by sawing followed by hand planing. Sand the edges to remove the sharp edges.

6. Mark the double mortise positions on the legs. Cut out the mortises, keeping them straight and square. Note the recesses for the tenon haunch and central tongue.

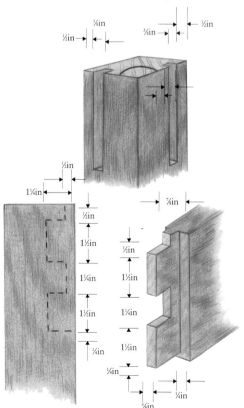

7. Mark the double tenons as shown on the side and end rails. Cut out the tenons

straight and square. Remember the haunch and central tongue (see page 145). Test fit the individual tenons into their respective mortises. Trim as required for a good fit.

8. Assemble the legs and the side and end rails without using glue, and check that everything fits well and is square.

9. Check the position of the cutout for the drawer, and the position and required length (including the stub tenons) of the two internal cross rails that support and strengthen the frame. Disassemble.

10. Mark the position of the drawer opening on the front side rail. Cut this out and clean up the edges. This opening should finish at 16 x 3½ inches.

11. Mark the position of the mortises for the cross rails on the inside surfaces of the side rails. Make sure that the cross rails will be parallel. Cut the mortises carefully, no more than ½ inch deep.

12. Mark the stub tenons on the cross rails. Cut them out and check them individually for a good fit. The cross rails should be just flush with the drawer opening.

13. Test assemble the complete frame, including the cross rails, which must be put in position first. Disassemble.

14. If the leg joints are to be additionally secured with wooden pins, these should be prepared at this stage (see page 145 for "draw boring").

15. Clean off all surface marks, then glue and assemble the frame. Assemble the cross rails first, then join the rails to the legs. Hold them with clamps or insert securing pegs. Check the frame is square, clean off surplus glue and leave until the glue has dried.

16. Prepare and attach the drawer runners. Screw these into place rather than gluing them. They should be just flush with the drawer opening and parallel to each other.

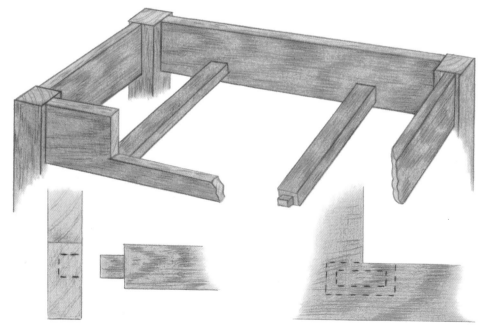

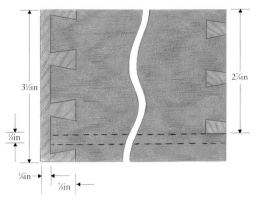

17. Make the drawer. It has lapped dovetails at the front and through dovetails at the back (see page 143). Plane the drawer front to a good, tight fit in the drawer opening. Cut the drawer back to the same length, or slightly less, and the side pieces to the same width as the front. Check that the ends are square and mark adjoining pieces.

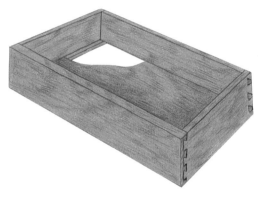

18. Cut the groove for the drawer bottom in the front piece and both side pieces. (See diagram at top of page.)

19. Mark and cut out the dovetail joints, the "tails" first, on each end of the side pieces. Use the measurements and proportions given above and see page 143 for method.

20. Mark out the dovetail "sockets" using the "tails" cut in step 19 as a template. Cut them out (see page 143 for method).

21. Test fit each joint, keeping all handling to a minimum, and adjust as necessary for a good fit. Assemble the drawer, without glue, and check for square. Disassemble and clean off any surface marks.

22. Apply glue and assemble the drawer. Clamp it together, check that it is square, and leave it to dry.

23. Measure the required size for the drawer bottom. The grain should run from side to side. Trim it to fit the groove at the front and sides (it slides underneath the back). The bottom is not glued, but is held in place by screwing or pinning where it slides under the drawer back.

24. When the drawer is dry, clean off in the joint areas. Try it for fit in the drawer opening. Adjust for a good sliding fit.

25. Assemble the drawer stops as shown – it is easier to do this before assembling the top.

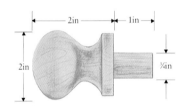

26. Make or buy a knob for the drawer. Drill a tight hole for the shaft and glue it in place. Secure it with a wedge if possible.

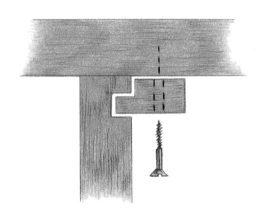

27. You can now attach the top. Using "buttons" is the usual method of doing this. These screw to the top, but are held in grooves in the side rails and are free to slide

in order to allow for any movement of the wood. The step of the button should be slightly less than the distance between the groove and the rail edge in order to keep the top pulled downward. Make sure the screws are not too long. Attach two buttons at each end and two along each side.

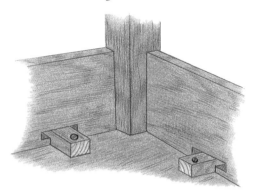

28. Before attaching the top, plane the top surface to a good finish. Plane its edges smooth and bevel over the top edges and corners. Then assemble as described in step 27.

29. The frame may be stained darker or left as it is and given a finish appropriate for its use (see pages 146-7). The pine top may also be given a clear finish; if it is to go in the kitchen, the top may be left untreated and kept clean by scrubbing.

Right - THIS SMALL TABLE, WITH ITS ELEGANT TAPERED LEGS AND USEFUL DRAWER, IS SIMILAR IN CONSTRUCTION TO THE SIDE TABLE. HERE, IT IS USED TO SUPPORT A MODERN READING LAMP, BUT ITS TIMELESS SIMPLICITY IS IN KEEPING WITH THE WOODEN PANELING ON THE WALL AND THE COLONIAL CARVER CHAIR.

Wood Outside

A liking for the country life implies a love of the outdoors, for the two concepts are inseparable. Naturalness and a lack of pretention are at the very heart of the notion of country style. And how better to feel close to nature – even if only at weekends when you can get a few days away from the concrete of the city streets – than being outside with the sun on your back and the good earth under your feet? And what better than the naturalness of wood to celebrate this affinity?

WOOD AS A BUILDING MATERIAL

Wood as a building material has a long association with mankind, from the simple, often temporary shelters of our early ancestors to the solidly permanent, wooden-frame buildings of medieval times; from the rough-hewn log cabins common in the high-forest regions of Europe, and used again and again by the colonial pioneers everywhere, to the weatherboarded, shingle-roofed houses typical of the east coast of North America. The early settlers built their homes using the material they found most readily at hand – and where there happened to be an abundance of trees, wood, of course, predominated. The manner in which they built, however, was strongly influenced by the traditions of their native homelands and also, to some extent, by the type and size of the local trees and the size and durability of the logs they yielded.

A TRANSITIONARY SPACE

Many of these ethnic building styles had one notable architectural feature in common, however – the porch, or veranda. In fact, *veranda* is a Hindi word, as is bungalow, which was absorbed into the language in the days of the British Raj in India. Built as a type of covered, but usually open-sided, extension to a house, the porch is where the inside meets the outside, and where the distinction between the two often becomes blurred.

The construction and character of the porch can vary enormously, from the rigidly formal to the strictly functional, from the rustic to the ramshackle. Where a porch is not regularly maintained by painting or preserving in some other fashion, its wood will soon begin to weather, taking on the textures and the muted, earthy colors of the surrounding countryside – thus strengthening the ever-present link with nature.

Depending on its geographical location or the season of the year, the porch may function as a much-used outdoor room – a playroom for the children, perhaps – or have only limited, more occasional use for entertaining. Where the climate is mild and the summers are long and hot, the porch provides essential shade and, being in regular use, will probably have its own permanent furniture and fixtures – like any other room of the house. Where the climate is less temperate,

Right - THIS AMISH FARMER'S LOG HOUSE, DATING FROM THE LATE 1730S, HAS BEEN MOVED TO CHESTER COUNTY, PENNSYLVANIA. THE STEEPLY PITCHED ROOF IS CLAD WITH RIVEN SHINGLES, THE WESTERN RED CEDAR FROM WHICH THEY WERE MADE NOW WEATHERED BY SUN, WIND, AND RAIN TO A PLEASING SILVER GRAY COLOR.

Far right - RUSTIC FURNITURE, TYPICAL OF THE TYPE ASSOCIATED WITH THE ADIRONDACK REGION OF NORTHERN NEW YORK STATE, FILLS THIS PORCH. THE FURNITURE, AND THE SUPPORTING CORNER POSTS OF THE BARE, WEATHERED TREE TRUNKS, BRINGS A FEELING OF THE FOREST CLOSER TO THE LIVING SPACE.

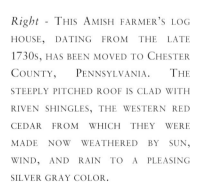

however, and the weather more uncertain, the porch will be more irregularly used and will need the type of furnishings that can be readily carried indoors and out.

WOODEN FURNITURE

A small table or bench has many uses outdoors and, in particular, the simple five-board bench suits a veranda or porch extremely well. It is easily made by assembling the prepared components, without requiring too many carpentry skills, and it was among the earliest pieces made by rural woodworkers in many different countries. Its method of construction makes it a very adaptable piece of furniture. It can be built in a variety of useful sizes, ranging from footstools to tables, and its inherent simplicity ranks it along with the best of traditional country style.

In most people's minds, the quintessential piece of porch furniture must be the rocking chair. A late 18th-century innovation, the rocking chair was at first known by the name *digestive chair*, an affirmation of its perceived use then and now. The admission by some unknown early devotee of the rocker that ". . . sometimes I rocks and thinks and sometimes I just rocks" encapsulates the totally relaxing image of the old rocking chair set out in some shady corner on the back porch.

Chairs that rock, and others that don't, are made in all shapes and sizes, and many styles are suitable for porch or outdoor use. It is a historical fact that Windsor chairs were originally much used outside in English gardens, and many were painted green for this specific purpose. And it appears that similar chairs were used in some London parks and cricket grounds up until about the turn of the 20th century. Another style of chair, the lath or ladderback Shaker-style chair with a simple woven seat, is eminently suitable for outdoor use and is frequently used in this way. The austere yet graceful shapes of these chairs are entirely in keeping with the simplicity of country life.

Chairs, benches, and other items of furniture made in what is generally known as the rustic style are also extremely popular as both porch and outdoor furniture, as well as in some situations indoors. Rustic style combines country living with natural history: part furniture, part tree, it is a synthesis of man and nature, a union of the maker's mind and the spirits of the forest.

Left - THIS TABLE CONVERTS TO A HIGHBACK SEAT; IT IS A NEW ENGLAND VERSION OF THE SO-CALLED MONK'S BENCH.

Above Right - WHAT COULD BE MORE INVITING THAN A ROCKING CHAIR SITTING ON A SHELTERED PORCH, THE VERY EPITOME OF EASE AND RELAXATION?

Below Right - A LADDERBACK CHAIR AND TABLE – STRAGGLERS FROM SUMMER – WAIT TO BE TAKEN INDOORS AS THE NEW ENGLAND FALL BEGINS IN EARNEST.

BIRD HOUSE

One of the additional pleasures of having a town garden, or of living in a more rural setting, is the relationship you can build up with the resident animals of the not-too-wild variety – especially small birds. Given regular inducements of food, birds will readily adopt your backyard as part of their feeding territory, even becoming quite regular in their visits to collect your daily offerings. Attracting birds into a yard – an urban one, one set among forests or farmland, or even to the window ledge of a city apartment – depends on more than just food, however. Equally important are the other necessities of life, such as water and shelter.

"Feeding the birds" can range from occasionally throwing out scraps of leftover food to keeping a specially installed bird table or other feeding devices regularly stocked. Catering for the birds' need for water is often managed with a bird bath, elaborate and decorative, or simple and utilitarian. The design doesn't matter to the birds – as long as it is not too restricted in width or too deep for the likely bathers – and should be of a style that matches the rest of the outdoor furniture.

Supplying shelter for birds – a simple place for roosting or nesting – is usually achieved by providing a nest box. Different species of bird have very different nesting requirements, and a little research will help guarantee that the nesting box you build and install will meet the needs of the garden birds you wish to attract. The boxes illustrated here, which form the

inspiration for this particular project, are intended to be used by hole-nesting birds such as tits, robins, and sparrows. But the size of the entrance hole is the critical deciding factor, since invasion by other species of birds, as well as mammalian and reptilian egg stealers, is not uncommon if the recommended dimension is exceeded.

Nest boxes for outdoors do not have to be finished to a particularly high degree and certainly not as artistically as the ones pictured. The birds will not mind if the construction lacks some sophistication and finesse, and an exterior that blends with the natural surroundings would probably be more to their liking, too. This project is an excellent starting point for the novice woodworker, since the birds will not be a critical audience. Simply use the correct materials and follow stage-by-stage the construction details carefully – and don't forget to get the dimensions of the entrance hole correct for the birds you want to attract to your bird house.

Of course, bird houses are not limited to being used outside. They also have obvious esthetic appeal, and this has been seized upon as an interesting interior design idea. They have become increasingly popular as decorative objects in the home, sometimes left in their natural state to bring something of the outdoors into a room or onto a porch, but more often painted in matte earth colors similar to those seen here. If you intend to encourage nesting birds, boxes must be put out by the New Year at the latest.

Above - THIS HIGHLY ORNATE BIRD CAGE, A CLOSE RELATION OF THE BIRD HOUSE, IS A CHARMING EXAMPLE OF SKILLFUL RUSTIC HANDIWORK. ALTHOUGH SIMPLY CONSTRUCTED, THE WEALTH OF SMALL DECORATIVE TOUCHES ADDS UP TO SOMETHING FAR MORE ELABORATE. YOU COULD USE THESE AS A SOURCE OF INSPIRATION WHEN IT COMES TO DECORATING YOUR OWN BIRD HOUSE.

Right - THE PORCH OF A LOG CABIN LOCATED IN NEW YORK STATE PROVIDES JUST THE RIGHT SETTING FOR A COLLECTION OF BIRD HOUSES OR BOXES. THESE WERE ALL MADE BY A FOLK ARTIST IN THE 1950s. ALTHOUGH THEY WERE DESIGNED TO HAVE AN ENTIRELY PRACTICAL FUNCTION, THEY DO LOOK DECIDEDLY DECORATIVE, TOO.

Above - THIS ATTRACTIVE BIRD HOUSE IS SUITABLE FOR HOLE-NESTING BIRDS.

ABILITY LEVEL: Novice

SIZE: 10 x 8 x 6 inches

MATERIALS: Pine
Piece of leather or sheet rubber

CUTTING LIST:
1 front
10 x 6 x ⅝ inches

1 back
10 x 6 x ⅝ inches

2 sides
7 x 5 x ⅝ inches

1 roof side
7½ x 6 x ⅝ inches

1 roof side
7 x 6 x ⅝ inches

1 floor
8 x 5 x ⅝ inches

Note: All pieces can be cut from a single length, 50 x 6 x ⅝ inches. A piece of floorboard would be suitable.

All measurements are given in inches.

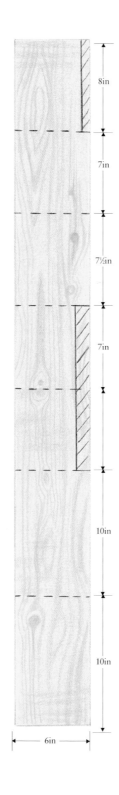

METHOD:

1. Begin by marking out the required pieces and saw to size. Mark each piece for its intended use so that there is no confusion later on.

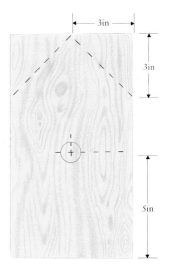

2. Mark out the roof line on the front piece and cut away the waste wood to make the required 45° slope. Mark the position of the entrance hole on the front piece and drill it to the recommended diameter, which is 1⅛ inches for small birds such as tits and robins and 1¼ inches for larger birds such as sparrows. If you don't have a drill of the right size, drill a series of small holes and enlarge them with a file. Smooth the edges of the finished hole.

Slotted hole for
hanging

3. Mark out the roof line on the back piece and cut away the waste wood to make the required 45° slope. Make a slotted hole in the back piece for hanging the finished box from a screw or nail.

4. Drill a couple of drainage holes in the floor piece of the box. About ¼ inch in diameter is adequate.

5. Mark and cut out a 45° chamfer on the top edge of each side piece of the box to follow the roof line.

6. Assemble the front, back, and side pieces, without glue, and check that the side chamfers align correctly. Adjust as necessary.

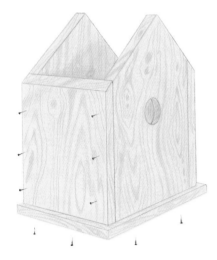

7. Carefully glue and then nail the front, back, and side pieces of the bird house together. Use a waterproof (outdoor) glue.

Take care when nailing not to split the wood (see page 141 for advice on nailing).

Leather or rubber for roof hinge

3in

6in

8. Put the floor piece into position. Note that there is an overhang to the front and sides. Glue and nail the floor into place, making sure that the structure remains square. Remove surplus glue and leave to dry.

9. Check the roof pieces for fit. Note how the longer piece overlaps the shorter. If all is well, glue and nail them into place.

10. Cover the roof joint with a strip of leather or sheet rubber. Attach this securely with large-headed nails or tacks.

11. If you want to be able to open the box for out-of-season cleaning, only nail the shorter half of the roof permanently into position.

Roof catch

Leave the other loose, with the leather or rubber acting as a hinge.

12. Secure the hinged half of the roof with a simple catch. The detail illustration shows how to make this from two small fence staples and a short piece of wire. Take care not to split the wood with the staples.

13. Perches beneath the entrance hole are not recommended, since they could encourage predators. If you wish to use one, insert a natural twig into a drilled hole.

14. Treat the finished nest box with a suitable wood preservative, carefully following the manufacturer's instructions and working in a well-ventilated area. Apply the wood preservative well in advance of hanging the box to allow the fumes to disperse. This also applies if you intend to paint the outside.

15. Site the box at least 6 feet above the ground and away from direct sunshine, preferably among trees or shrubs. Put the box out many weeks before the breeding season to allow birds to become accustomed to its presence in their territory.

From early times, the chair has always been a symbol of authority rather than merely something to sit on. For chieftains to chairmen, it has indicated status – and even today, from corporate body to village committee, the chairperson is recognized as being in charge. Until about the middle of the 16th century, chairs were a rarity; only the lord of the manor or the head of the family had one – everybody else made do with stools, benches, or forms.

The most obvious difference between these "low-status" seats and chairs is that they are backless, but the difference among them is not always so clear. A stool is a movable seat for one person, but if it is extended to accommodate more than one, it becomes either a bench or a form. Although these last two terms are often used synonymously, a bench was originally a substantial stationary seat, while a form is generally of lighter construction and is movable. In the British House of Commons, Members of Parliament sit on benches, and the more junior Members, who sit at the back, are known as backbenchers. And it is from the use of the extended stool – the form – in the medieval school hall, where pupils sat in strict order of progress on the first, second or third form, that school classes or grades are in some places in Britain still referred to as *forms*.

Stools as well as extended stools were constructed in different ways, from variations on the peg-leg type, like the milking stool (see page 26), to the elaborate, turned and carved "joyned" stool and bench. An early version was the trestle construction, some of these not unlike the tables of the time, consisting of a board mounted on two solid end pieces that were braced in some way – sometimes centrally but, more usually, by side pieces. The ends might be either tenoned through the top and secured by wedging or made by a more simple method in which the five components are pegged, screwed, or nailed together.

This type of bench (or form) was common across Europe and North America, and was most often made in pine and then painted. It was a popular piece of furniture for use both indoors and out. Its attraction lies in the ready availability of the raw material, the fact that it requires little in the way of woodworking skills, and only the simplest of tools are needed. The method of construction means that the bench can be made in an infinite variety of sizes and adapted to fulfil a number of functions, from the smallest child's stool to an extended bench suitable for seating several adults. By increasing its height, the bench may be turned into a small table that, in style, is particularly suited for use in the garden or out on the porch or verandah. The dimensions given here are for a generous-sized two-seater, but it could easily be extended to seat three people or reduced to make a useful stool for one person.

Left - THE VERSATILITY IN SIZE AND DESIGN OF THE FIVE-BOARD BENCH IS CLEARLY SEEN HERE. THESE PORCH BENCHES AND STOOLS ARE MOSTLY MADE OF PINE, THEIR WELL-WORN PAINTWORK TESTIMONY TO THEIR POPULARITY AND CONTINUING USE.

Above - A SMALL BENCH – PERHAPS ORIGINALLY DESIGNED AS A STOOL FOR A CHILD – HAS BEEN TURNED INTO A USEFUL LOW BENCH-TABLE FOR A BATHROOM. THE ANTIQUE WOODEN CARRIER PERCHED ON TOP, ORIGINALLY A CARRIER FOR FLATWARE, SERVES AS A HOLD-ALL FOR BATHROOM ACCESSORIES.

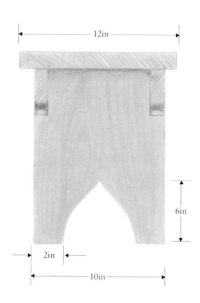

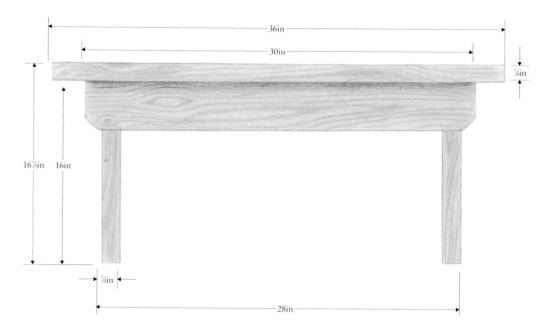

ABILITY LEVEL: Novice

SIZE: 36 x 16⅞ x 12 inches

MATERIALS: Pine or any hardwood

CUTTING LIST:
1 top
36 x 12 x ⅞ inches

2 ends
16 x 10 x ⅞ inches

2 sides
30 x 4 x ⅞ inches

See template pattern on page 152 for cutting legs.

Note: If the bench is to be used in the yard or on a porch, use waterproof glue when assembling the final pieces.

All measurements are given in inches.

METHOD:

1. Select and prepare all the material using the dimensions given. If necessary, make up the 12-inch widths by edge-joining narrower boards (see page 141).

2. Cut out the shapes of the two end pieces (see page 152 for template pattern), or cut them out to a shape of your own design.

3. Cut the housings for the side rails as shown. Cut these to suit the exact dimensions of the side pieces in case these differ from those given in the cutting list. These housing joints, when well made and glued and nailed, or screwed, together, add considerably to the rigidity of the bench.

4. Now shape the ends of the side rails as shown and smooth off all sawn edges and sharp corners.

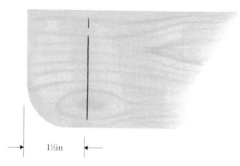

5. Mark pencil guidelines 1½ inches in and square across on each end of the side rails as an aid to nailing or screwing. Note the 1-inch overlap over the end pieces. This extra length reduces the risk of splitting when the side rails are joined to the end pieces.

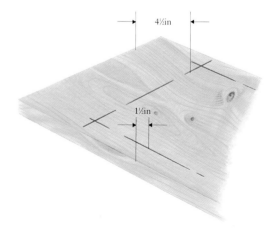

6. Mark pencil guidelines square across the top of the bench, 4½ inches in from each end and parallel to the edge, 1½ inches in from each edge. These, too, are an aid to nailing or screwing.

7. The bench can be nailed together in traditional fashion, using oval or finishing nails. Be careful not to split the wood, especially when attaching the side rails (see page 141 for advice). Set the nail heads below the surface and fill the indentations.

8. As an alternative, you can join the bench together using countersunk screws. Drill and counterbore the holes to accommodate the screws and the wooden plugs glued in on top to conceal them (see page 141). If hardwood is used, the bench must be screwed together.

9. Begin assembly by joining the side rails to the end pieces. Nail or screw as required. Apply glue first to strengthen the joints.

10. Check that the basic frame remains square and then wipe off surplus glue and leave it to dry.

11. Check that the top will fit correctly. Line up the pencil guidelines to give about a 4-inch overhang at each end and a 1-inch overhang over each side piece.

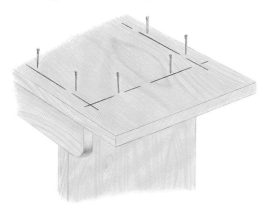

12. Using the pencil lines as a guide, nail or screw into both ends and side pieces. The nails or screws will hold better in the side rails than in the end grain of the end pieces.

13. Set all nail heads below the surface and fill the indentations, or glue and plug the counterbored screw holes.

14. Remove the pencil marks and sand all surfaces clean. Round over all sharp edges, especially those on the top of the seat.

15. Finish according to your choice by clear varnishing, staining, or painting (see pages 146-7 for advice on finishes). If the bench is to be used regularly outdoors, the application of a suitable wood preservative will prolong the life of the bench, especially if pine was used in its construction.

Below - OFFERING RELIEF FROM THE HEAT OF THE DAY, AND THE USUAL SEASONAL GARDEN CHORES, THIS SHADY BENCH IS SUFFICIENTLY INFORMAL IN DESIGN TO FIND FAVOR IN ANY STYLE OF GARDEN.

The easiest definition of whirligigs is that they are a type of wind-driven toy. This, however, is a fairly loose definition, for they are much more than that. Part toy, part machine, they can vary from the very simple to the most complex; from a single moving object or figure to a whole orchestra (literally) of movement. Activated by all types of mechanisms – by direct drive or through a series of cams and cranks – they can be driven by an assortment of different propeller designs, such as single-blade, four-blade, and multiblade types. Whether they are whimsical weather vanes or wind-powered wonderments, they are most often painted in bright colors. Their use is nonfunctional, and their intention is simply to entertain and delight.

Whirligigs were particularly popular in the United States during the 19th century, and they are now enjoying something of a revival once more: their origins, however, remain a bit of a mystery. The name itself is derived from a combination of two Old Norse words: *whirl,* meaning to spin about, and *gig,* to turn or shake about. In the 15th century, whirligig, or whirlygigge, was the name given to the toy that we now know as the spinning top and also to the first merry-go-rounds at English country fairs. Folded paper pinwheels on sticks, sold as novelty toys at these fairs, and model or toy windmills have also been known at one period or another as whirligigs, while the whirligig beetle is the common name in some localities for a whole

family of flat-bodied water beetles that skim and whirl around on the surface of still water. It was also the name given to a type of revolving punishment cage used to hold criminals in the early part of the 15th century, and in the 19th century the now common revolving office chair was called a whirligig long before it became known as the swivel chair. And the name has literary connections, too – William Shakespeare, in *Twelfth Night,* refers to "the whirligig of time." The American short story writer O. Henry (William Sydney Porter) called one of his books *Whirligigs,* an apt title for a collection of stories that twist and turn about and typically have surprise endings.

The colorful and animated wind-driven devices that we now call whirligigs may well have had an Asian ancestry, probably introduced from the Far East, perhaps by the Chinese, who are credited with the invention of both the windmill and the kite. Nothing is authentically documented, however. Settlers from the East to North America no doubt brought many different designs for kites, windmills, and whirligigs with them, and, in the course of time, the figures on the whirligigs and the actions they performed took on a distinctive style that is unique to North America. In the past, whirligigs have played an important role in the lives of hardworking country folk, providing both a recreational occupation for creative woodworking skills and a welcome outlet for an obviously rich sense of humor.

Above - THE WEATHER VANE IS A CLOSE RELATION OF THE WHIRLIGIG, AND THE CROWING ROOSTER IS A FAVORITE MOTIF IN THEIR MAKING. MADE FROM WOOD OR METAL, THESE BRIGHTLY PAINTED IMAGES ARE OFTEN USED AS ORNAMENTS IN THE COUNTRY-STYLE INTERIOR.

Right - THE THEME OF THIS COLORFUL WHIRLIGIG, PICTURED HERE AGAINST A BACKGROUND OF RIPENING CORN, IS "JACK CHOPPING WOOD." SUCH CHARACTERIZATION WAS A FEATURE OF MANY SUCH CONSTRUCTIONS, AND IT IS THIS THAT ENDEARS THEM TO MODERN COLLECTORS.

ABILITY LEVEL: Novice/Intermediate

SIZE: 20 x 18 x 1½ inches

MATERIALS: Wood, waterproof plywood, metal

CUTTING LIST:
Wood
1 platform
16 x 1 x ⅞ inches

1 pivot block
3 x 1 x ⅞ inches

1 drive shaft block
3 x 1½ x ⅞ inches

1 propeller hub
3 x 3 x 1 inches

4 pieces dowel
5 x ½-inch diameter

1 small wooden bead

Waterproof plywood (or wood)
Figure parts, ax, propeller blades, tail, chopping block
24 x 12 x ¼ inches

Metal
1 piece threaded rod
5½ x ¼-inch diameter

6 nuts and washers
¼-inch diameter (to suit rod)

1 large flange washer
¼ x 1½ inch OD

1 piece brass tubing
5 x ⁵⁄₁₆ inch OD

1 machine screw
2 x ³⁄₁₆-inch diameter

1 nut and 4 washers to suit machine screw

1 small screw eye, assorted nails, and screws for assembly

1 piece of stiff wire for connecting rod

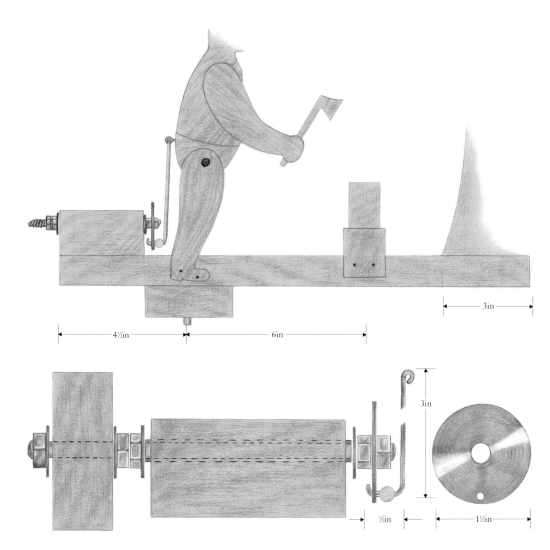

Notes: Use waterproof glue for assembly. The threaded rod (drive shaft) should run freely inside the brass tubing. The drive mechanism will need a drop of oil periodically; applying petroleum jelly to the drive shaft before assembly is a useful long-term precaution.

OD = outside diameter.

See template patterns on page 154.

All measurements are given in inches.

METHOD:

1. Using the full-sized templates on page 154, mark and cut out all of the parts for the figure. Cut one body, two waists, two legs, and two arms. Clean up all sawn edges.

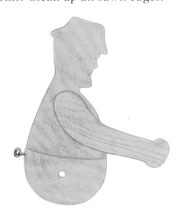

2. Glue the arms and waists to the body, one on each side as shown. Clamp the work until the glue is dry.

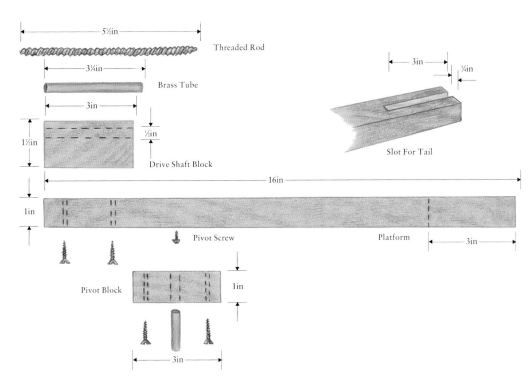

3. When dry, drill the figure pivot hole through to clear the ³⁄₁₆-inch machine screw. Align and drill corresponding holes through the legs at the same time.

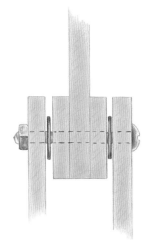

4. Attach the legs to the figure using the machine screw, placing the washers as shown to reduce friction. Check the movement is free, then put it aside until later.

5. Mark and cut out the remaining plywood/wood components using the templates on page 154. Clean up the sawn edges.

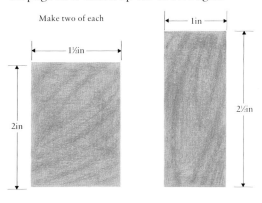

6. From the same material, cut out the chopping block parts and glue these together as shown on the right.

7. Cut the platform, drive shaft block, and pivot block to length. Make a ¼-inch slot in one end of the platform for the tail to be attached later. Then carefully drill a ⁵⁄₁₆-inch diameter hole through the length of the drive shaft block.

8. Cut a 3¼-inch length of the brass tubing and push this into the hole drilled in the drive shaft block, leaving equal lengths of tubing protruding from each end. File the ends of the tube smooth.

9. Drill a ⅛-inch hole in the outer edge of the large flange washer for the connecting rod attachment. Place the threaded rod through the brass tube and assemble the washers and nuts, large flange washer, and lock nut, as shown. Don't overtighten. Test that the shaft rotates freely.

10. Drill a hole ⁵⁄₁₆ inch in diameter through the center of the pivot block and push the remainder of the brass tubing into the hole to check that it fits.

11. Now screw and glue the two blocks to the platform in the positions shown on the previous page. To reduce friction in the pivot block when it is mounted, position a round headed screw in the underside of the platform, as shown above, before attaching the pivot block.

12. Glue and nail the figure to the platform in the position indicated. Screw the small eye into the back of the figure at the point shown, and then cut and bend the connecting rod wire, using the dimensions given as a guide only. Adjust as necessary. Put the small bead in place; this keeps the connecting rod clear of the end of the drive shaft. Attach the connecting rod to the flange washer and to the figure.

13. Test the movements of the drive shaft and figure and adjust the length of the connecting rod as necessary.

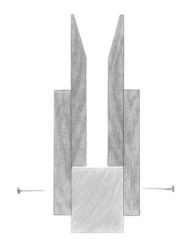

14. Make a deep V-shaped groove in the top of the chopping block and place it in position, without using glue, on the platform. Next, temporarily attach the ax between the figure's hands. Rotate the drive shaft and test the movement of the ax in relation to the chopping block. The ax should go partway into the groove without actually touching it anywhere. Adjust the positions of the ax and block as necessary and then glue and pin them into place.

15. Make the four-bladed propeller as shown. The dimensions of the hub, propeller blades, and other details are given with the templates (see page 154).

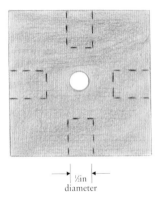

½in
diameter

16. It is easiest to drill the holes while the hub is still square. Carefully mark and drill the ⁵⁄₁₆-inch diameter center hole right through the wood, and then mark and drill the ½-inch diameter propeller arm holes to a depth of ¾ inch. Either cut the hub to shape or leave it square.

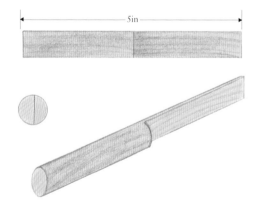

5in

17 After checking that the arm dowels fit in the holes drilled in the hub, cut the arm dowels halfway through, as shown. The flat surfaces formed by this shaping accommodate the propeller blades. The lower edges of the blades should not be closer to the hub center than 3 inches.

18. Glue the individual blades in position and secure them with small brads, taking care not to split the dowels (see page 141 for advice). Allow the glue to dry before going on to the next step.

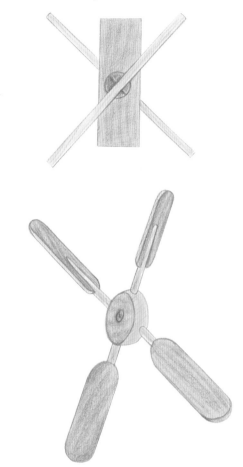

19. Insert the arms into their respective holes in the hub, without using glue. Rotate the arms so that pairs of blades are at opposite angles of about 45° to each other on either side of the hub. Glue the arms into position. Test the propeller for balance, using a spare piece of rod or a suitable-sized nail as a free pivot. If one blade is heavier than the rest, it will always come to a stop at the bottom. Remove surplus wood from the blades until the balance is correct. Then attach the propeller to the drive shaft; secure it with the nut and lock nut.

20. Fit, glue, and nail the tail into the tail slot already cut in the platform. The tail is the mechanism that helps to keep the propeller facing into the wind. When the glue is dry, test the mechanism outside in the wind and make adjustments as necessary.

21. If the whirligig is to be used outdoors, you must protect it with a good-quality exterior paint over a sound undercoat. Choose a realistic color scheme, like the one shown on page 59, which uses only earth colors and is in keeping with the style of the project. Make sure that no paint is allowed to clog the working parts.

22. When the paint is dry, mount the whirligig on a suitable pivot, such as a steel rod or a nail driven into a stand or post.

23. The drive mechanism on the whirligig will need a drop of oil from time to time to ensure that it continues to work smoothly; applying a light grease (petroleum jelly) to the drive shaft before assembly is a useful long-term precaution.

Right - A FINE COLLECTION OF WHIRLIGIGS STANDS SENTINEL OVER THE PORCH OF A NORTH AMERICAN COUNTRY HOME IN NEW YORK STATE, EACH DEVICE PERCHED ON TOP OF ITS OWN POST TO CATCH THE SLIGHTEST BREEZE. THIS EXCELLENT LOCATION MEANS THAT THEY ARE EASILY ENJOYED BY ANYONE VENTURING TO SIT OUTSIDE AND PROVIDE A PERMANENT DISPLAY OF COLOR AND MOVEMENT. NOTE THE BRIGHT HUES THAT HAVE BEEN USED FOR THEIR DECORATION – THERE IS NO NEED TO LIMIT YOURSELF TO SOBER EARTH COLORS IF BRIGHT AND CHEERFUL IS WHAT YOU PREFER. THE RESULT IS STILL AUTHENTIC.

ROCKING CHAIR

Perhaps more than any other single item of household furniture, the rocking chair evokes the strongest feeling of the past and the comfort of country living. The origin of the rocking chair is obscure, but it seems to have appeared throughout Europe and North America toward the end of the 18th century. In America, rocking chairs became extremely popular, especially for after-dinner relaxation, and they were apparently given the name "digestive chairs." However, in Victorian England, rocking chairs were considered "socially unacceptable" and were approved only on medical grounds – presumably as an aid to digestion!

Their acceptance and widespread popularity in the United States led to the development of specially designed rocking chairs such as the Boston Rocker, and the Shaker communities also designed many chairs to rock. The much-exported Thonet line of bentwood furniture from Austria included several elaborate rocking chairs in which the rockers were an integral part of the construction. In Britain, there appear to have been few, if any, chairs that were made specifically for rocking. Instead, during the late 19th century, chairs which were normally stationary could have rockers added to them at the request of the purchaser, and trade catalogs of the period offered to attach rockers at the cost of an extra shilling.

To understand the small size of the rocking chair on the left in this picture, we have to appreciate the extent to which domestic living has changed over the centuries. From ancient times, family and home life was concentrated around the hearth because the open fireplace was the source of light as well as heat; it was where people cooked, ate, and gathered together to keep warm, talk, and make music. Because the fire was on a low level, seat heights were correspondingly low, and because there was often a need to accommodate as many people as possible around the fire, chairs were designed to take up minimum space. Later, the table replaced the hearth as a gathering point, and chair seat heights were raised to allow for sitting at the table, and they became both taller and bulkier. However, small hearth culture chairs are still found throughout Europe and North America. This project explains how to make a small rocking chair.

Left - THE FURNITURE ON THIS PORCH INCLUDES THE SMALL ROCKING CHAIR DESCRIBED IN THE FOLLOWING PROJECT. THE BENTWOOD CHAIRS, COMMONLY MADE IN THE SOUTHERN UNITED STATES, ARE MADE FROM GREEN (UNSEASONED), SUPPLE, FAST-GROWING WOODS SUCH AS WILLOW AND COTTONWOOD.

ABILITY LEVEL: Intermediate

SIZE: 34 x 16 x 16 inches

MATERIALS: Ash, Beech, Maple

CUTTING LIST:

2 back uprights
31 x 2 x 1¼ inches

2 front legs
14 x 2 x 1¼ inches

(Cut the 2 back uprights and 2 front legs
from 2 pieces of wood:
31 x 5 x 1¼ inches)

2 seat rails
15 x 2 x 1 inches

7 stretcher rails
15 x 1⅛ x 1⅛ inches

1 back rail
15 x 1½ x 1 inches

1 comb (cut from 1 piece)
16 x 4 x 3 inches

1 seat (made from 3 pieces)
17 x 4 x 1 inches

2 rockers (cut from 1 piece)
30 x 6 x 1½ inches

See template patterns on page 155 for
comb and rockers.

All measurements are given in inches.

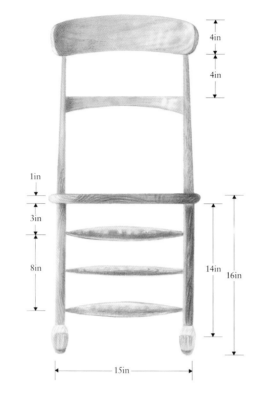

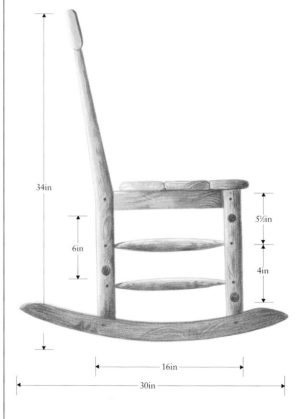

METHOD:

Construction of this chair is simplified if the
sequence of making two separate side
"units" and then joining these together with
cross rails is followed.

1. Cut out the two back uprights (see pattern
on page 155). Clean up sawn surfaces: leave
rectangular below seat level; above, smooth
over the outside edges only and round the
top to 1-inch diameter.

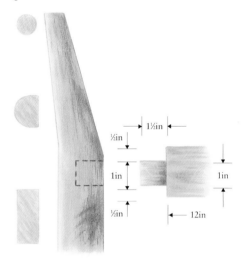

2. Make the two front legs (see pattern on
page 155) and clean up sawn surfaces.

3. Mark and cut out mortises for the seat
rails in the back uprights and front legs (see
page 144 for mortise and tenon joint).

4. Check that the seat rails are of correct and
equal length; mark and cut out tenons to fit
mortises. Check for a snug fit.

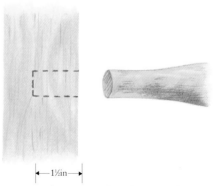

5. Make four round side-stretcher rails to
length and 1-inch diameter by turning or
otherwise (see page 138). Form ¾-inch diameter tenon joints at each end.

6. Mark the position of the stretcher rails on the inside edges of the front legs and leg portion of the back uprights. Drill these joint sockets to measure ¾-inch diameter and 1¼ inch deep.

7. Test fit the side stretcher rails individually to make sure that they fit properly into the leg sockets.

8. Assemble the dry (unglued) back uprights, front legs, seat rails, and side stretcher rails to make two separate side "units."

9. Cut out a pair of rockers (see pattern on page 155). Clean up sawn surfaces.

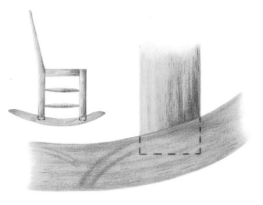

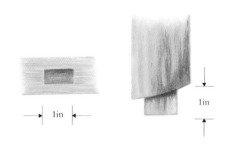

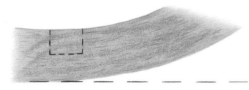

10. With the side "units" lying on a flat surface, place a rocker onto each as shown, and mark the top curve of the rocker on the bottom end of each leg. Also mark the position of mortises for leg tenons on each rocker.

11. Cut leg mortises into each rocker. Keep the joint vertical to a flat surface and not to the rocker surface.

12. Mark and cut out the leg tenons, scribing the shoulder of each joint to the marked line (see step 10) to obtain a close fit with the top surface of the rocker.

13. Check the fit of the tenons into the mortises in the rockers. Disassemble for the next stages.

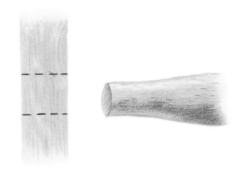

14. Make 3 round cross stretcher rails to the required length and 1-inch diameter (see page 138 for advice on shaping). Form ¾-inch round tenon joints at each end.

15. Mark the position of these rails on the outside surfaces of the legs and drill through at ¾ inch. Test fit the rails.

16. Mark the position of the mortises in the back uprights for the back cross rail. Cut out these mortises.

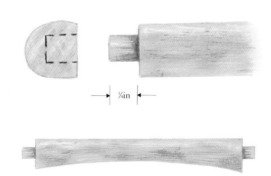

17. Mark and cut out the stub tenons on the ends of the back cross rail. Hollow the front surface of the rail for added comfort, as shown.

18. Cut out the comb from the pattern (see page 155). Clean up sawn surfaces, but to make drilling easier in the next step, leave rounding over the top edge and ends until after the joint sockets have been made.

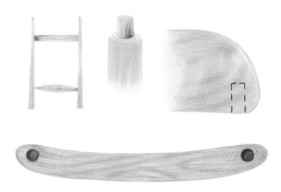

19. Temporarily assemble the back uprights and cross rails to check the width between the top round tenons. Mark this measurement on the underside of the comb and drill these joint sockets ¾ inch and 1 inch deep.

20. Form a ¾-inch shouldered round tenon on top of each back upright and try the comb for a good fit.

21. Following the pattern, assemble the seat from pieces, which may be edge-glued together or left separate. Round over the front edge.

22. To assemble the chair, begin by gluing and assembling the two side "units," including the rockers. Secure the joints by pegging (see page 145).

23. Join the two side "units" together by adding the cross rails. Note that these go through the back uprights and front legs. Secure by pegging and cut joints flush, if they are protruding.

24. Attach the comb to the back upright tenons.

25. Attach the seat boards by nailing or screwing into the side seat rails. Set nails or countersink screws below the surface and fill the indentations.

26. The chair may be finished by any of the methods described on pages 146-7.

RUSTIC CHAIR

Wherever there is thriving woodland, you will find young sapling trees. They are the result of natural regeneration, regrowth after a forest fire, perhaps, or the natural cycle of recovery following the clearance of mature trees by managed felling. In some woodland management systems, coppicing – the cutting of mature trees to encourage multistemmed regrowth – is a productive means of producing wood on a regular crop basis. Historically, these straight stems have been used in a variety of ways.

In the past, as well as on a small scale today, young tree stems were used for fencing, barn partitions, sheep hurdles, and fodder racks, and it was but a short step – where conditions required or poverty made necessary – to use this versatile material for simple, rustic furniture. Much the same methods of construction were employed – round tenons whittled on the end of round rails and secured into holes bored into joining pieces or, where components crossed each other, bound with cords or strips of bark. Nails might sometimes be used, but they were not always available and were expensive to buy when they were. Basic furniture, such as beds, tables, stools, and chairs, were all made in this way; and some folk styles today in Eastern Europe, Scandinavia, and North America still use similar forms of construction.

It was in the newly established colonies of 17th-century North America that this furniture really proliferated. Virgin forests provided an abundance of materials for building purposes, and the early pioneers were quick to take advantage of such a convenient and seemingly endless supply of wood. The first furniture would have been made from this same source, and it served its purpose well until replaced or relegated to a secondary role, usually as outdoor furniture, by the requirements of fashion and social change.

Interestingly, it is as the result of this social change and the growing pressures of urbanization that a revival of interest in the rustic furniture style has taken place. The organic feel of the style, its tactile surfaces, and the decorative qualities of the wood and the way it is used provide the ideal complement to a back-to-nature decor.

Right - A GALLERY OF RUSTIC-STYLE CHAIRS THAT ARE IDEAL FOR USE IN THE BACKYARD OR TO RELAX IN ON A COUNTRY PORCH. ALL THESE CHAIRS ARE FROM NORTH AMERICA EXCEPT FOR THE ONE SHOWN CENTER TOP. THIS TWIG CHAIR WAS MADE BY THE AUTHOR, AND DETAILS OF ITS CONSTRUCTION ARE GIVEN IN THE PROJECT THAT FOLLOWS.

ABILITY LEVEL: Intermediate

SIZE: 43 x 20 x 18 inches

MATERIALS: Young growth of Hazel, Birch, or Ash

CUTTING LIST:
2 back uprights
43 x 2-inch diameter

2 front uprights
28 x 2-inch diameter

2 back rails
19 x 1½-inch diameter

2 front rails
19 x 1½-inch diameter

4 side rails
18 x 1½-inch diameter

2 arms
22 x 1¾-inch diameter

1 comb
23 x 1¾-inch diameter

6 back sticks
24 x 1-inch diameter

3 "H" pieces
10 x 1-inch diameter

10 seat pieces
21½ x 1½-inch diameter

Notes: Diameters are approximate only and are given as a guide when gathering materials. Initially, cut pieces generously overlength and allow them to season (dry) before using them. The ends will probably split during the drying process.

   If the chair is to be used in the yard or on a porch, use a waterproof glue when assembling the final pieces.

All measurements are given in inches.

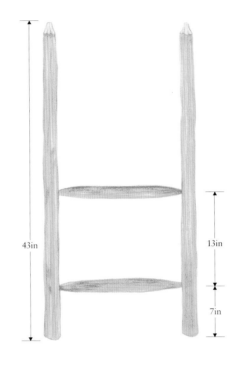

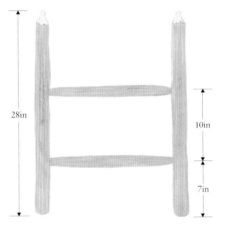

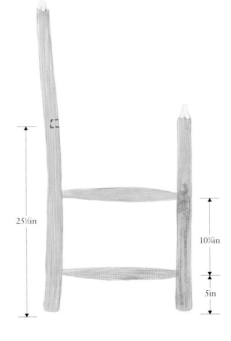

METHOD:

1. Select material according to its length and diameter. Choose back uprights that have a slight backward curve; all other pieces should be as straight as possible. When all pieces are thoroughly seasoned, cut everything to length. Remove the bark if you prefer, using a drawknife.

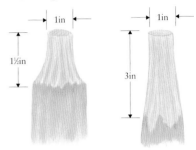

2. The chair is made in the form of two "ladders," back and front, of different lengths, joined together using side rails. This greatly simplifies the construction process. First, shape the top ends of both back and front uprights to form round tenons of 1-inch diameter. These are for the back comb and arms, respectively. Use a chisel, abrasives, drawknife or spokeshave to form the tenons.

3. Now mark and drill the joint sockets in the two back uprights to accommodate the two back rails. Do the same in the front uprights for the two front rails. Drill these sockets to a depth and diameter of 1 inch. Then shape the ends of the back and front rails to form round tenons, 1 inch in diameter, to fit the drilled sockets.

4. Assemble the front and back "ladders," without using glue, by fitting the rails into the uprights. Make sure the joints go in to their full depth. Mark the component pieces for their correct positions. Disassemble.

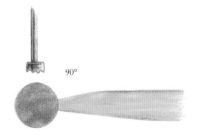

5. Mark the positions of the side rails on the back and front uprights and drill these to a depth and diameter of 1 inch, and at right angles to those previously drilled.

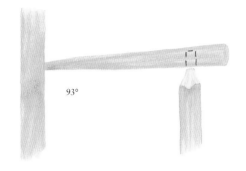

93°

6. Now mark and drill the sockets to hold the arms. These angle slightly upward, as shown, to allow for the slope of the arms. Next, shape the ends of the side rails (see step 3) to form 1-inch diameter tenons. Test fit rails in their respective sockets, making sure they enter to their full depth.

7. Reassemble the front and back "ladders," without gluing. Join them to the side rails to make the basic chair frame. Check that the chair stands without rocking. If necessary, use a soft mallet to tap the joints fully home.

8. Now mark the positions of the other components in the following order, although the measurements given are only a guide and may differ from chair to chair.

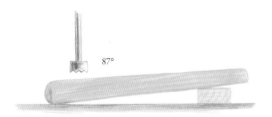

87°

9. First, shape the joint end of each of the arms to a diameter of 1 inch and fit them into the previously drilled sockets in the back uprights. Make sure they enter to their full depth and, while they are in place, mark the positions for drilling the front arm sockets to fit the tenons already made on the top of each front upright. Next, drill the arms at the marked positions to a depth and diameter of 1 inch and test fit the components. Drill these sockets at a slight angle to allow for the slope of the arms. Round over or bevel the front end of each arm.

10. Mark the position of the sockets in the back comb to fit the tenons on the top of each back upright. Drill these to a depth and diameter of 1 inch and test fit the components. Round over or bevel the ends.

18½in

2½in approx

11. Mark the positions of the sockets for the six back sticks on the top surface of the back rail and the underside of the back comb. Space these out equally, about 2½ inches apart, but check this on your own chair.

12. Mark the position of the vertical pieces of the front "H" on the top and bottom front rails, at the places shown. Disassemble basic frame. Drill back stick sockets to a diameter of ⅝ inch and a depth of ¼ inch.

4in   4in

13. Drill the front "H" sockets in the top and bottom front rails, to a diameter of ⅝ inch

and a depth of ¼ inch. Also drill the sockets for the cross piece.

14. Shape the ends of the back sticks to form ⅝-inch diameter round tenons. Test these in turn for fit in the drilled sockets. Then assemble the entire back "ladder," without gluing. Check for fit and squareness.

15. Shape the ends of the "H" pieces and try them for fit in the previously drilled sockets. Some adjustment of length may be needed. Without gluing, fit the front "H" into the front rails, assemble the entire front "ladder," and check for fit and squareness.

16. Without gluing, join the front and back "ladders" together with the side rails and put the arms into position. Check the complete chair goes together properly, then disassemble ready for gluing. First, glue together the back "ladder" and the front "ladder." Check that all joints fit to their full depth and that all is square. Add the side rails, then the arms. Make sure the joints fit to their full depth. Check the assembled chair stands upright on a level surface. You may want to peg the arms and the top front and top side rails (see page 145) for extra strength.

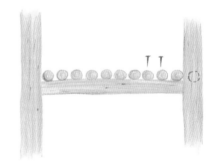

17. The seat consists of several separate pieces of wood placed side by side across the side seat rails, their tops level with the top front rail. Nail them into place, using a single oval or finishing nail at each end. To avoid splitting the wood, drill a small hole in each piece first, then set the nail heads below the surface.

18. Give the completed chair an oil finish or treat it with two or three coats of thinned polyurethane varnish. The use of a suitable wood preservative is recommended. (See pages 146-7 for advice on finishes.)

Kitchens & Dining Rooms

Much of the appeal of the country kitchen lies in its integrity and functional simplicity and in the kitchen's symbolic role as the heart of the house. Represented by strong, warm, time-toned colors and textures, everything is as well made as it is well used. There is little pretense of conformity, and you will find few "rules" regarding style.

Wood frequently predominated in these kitchen interiors, for it was discovered long ago that wood was the material most suited to the purpose. Furniture, implements, utensils, even the very fabric of the walls and ceiling, were often made entirely from wood. Today a fairly authentic note can be achieved by using tongue-and-groove planking on walls and possibly the ceiling, too. Paint it in a suitable earthy color, and you have the ideal backdrop for a country-style kitchen. Choose furniture that continues the theme – for example, a scrubbed pine table, a selection of simply constructed chairs, mix-and-match cabinets, and a basic hutch. Hang cheerful gingham or plaid curtains at the window, then decorate the walls and hutch with an eclectic mixture of old and new kitchenware, rural artefacts and anything else that appeals.

THE RURAL KITCHEN

In contrast to the crowded, gadget-packed kitchens we are familiar with today, it is difficult to imagine just how sparsely furnished and equipped were the kitchens of our ancestors. In those times, the kitchen of a farm worker, for example, would have contained little more than a sturdy table for food preparation, supplemented by a storage cupboard and perhaps a wall-hung pot shelf. Until the advent of the separate dining room, sometime in the 18th century, all meals would have been taken at the kitchen table, too, and for this purpose a few chairs or a bench would have been provided. In homes where there were large families, far more common than it is today, it is unlikely there would even have been enough seats to go around, and some, usually the younger family members, would have eaten their food standing up or squatting on the floor.

Central to the kitchen was the fireplace or open hearth, with the fire often being the only source of heat and the principal source of light after sunset. Since it was vital to the well-being and comfort of the entire household, laying the fire was the first task every morning.

Below, Right & Left - PLAIN WOODEN BENCHES PROVIDE USEFUL SEATING AT THE TABLE IN THE KITCHEN OR DINING ROOM AND SAVE SPACE, TOO. THE TWO BENCHES SHOWN HERE ARE COUNTRY MADE, THEIR LEGS BRACED FOR STRENGTH IN DIFFERENT BUT EQUALLY SUPPORTIVE WAYS.

Right - PRODUCE FROM THE GARDEN, HUNG TO DRY FROM A RACK, AND A DECORATIVE WITCH'S BROOM PROPPED IN THE CORNER BRING A TOUCH OF THE OUTDOORS TO THIS MODERN COUNTRY-STYLE KITCHEN WITH ITS NATURAL WOOD TONES AND SIMPLY DESIGNED FURNITURE.

When the log cabins of the early American settlers were being built, the stone fireplace and chimney were the first elements of the building to be constructed, and the remainder of the building was then put up around them.

All cooking was done in, on, or over an open fire, and while it was fueled by wood, hearths and cooking methods remained largely unchanged for centuries. It was not until the 19th century, when coal became widely available, that the hearth changed considerably. Because coal needs a constant supply of air in order to burn properly, it has to be contained in some type of raised iron basket or grate in order to create a better draft. This, in turn, led to the introduction of various types of enclosed, cast-iron constructions known as kitchen ranges, or stoves. These provided a means of cooking not only directly over the fire itself but also indirectly on a metal hot plate. An oven was also provided, as well as a side or back boiler, which supplied hot water.

Made to fit into the space previously occupied by the old hearths, kitchen ranges were literally bricked into the open fireplaces, which gradually fell out of favor, except in the poorest or most isolated of rural households. Smaller, freestanding kitchen ranges, known as portable stoves, which were supported on four legs and had an iron pipe to act as a flue, were an American innovation. Until the Great Exhibition in London, England, in 1851, these portable stoves were not available in Europe.

TABLE DESIGNS

The cottages and larger houses of more prosperous rural dwellers – those of a skilled artisan, local businessman, or tenant farmer, for example – would have had a sizable kitchen-dining room and some additional pieces of furniture. With more space available, there would have been room for a big table, and no doubt, enough seats for everybody in the family. Some early kitchen/dining tables were really massive affairs, sturdily built to last through several generations of use, and abuse. Some of them, in fact, are still with us today (together with many more reproductions of varying quality), which testifies to their fitness of purpose and the excellence of their construction.

Large numbers of kitchen/dining tables had tops made from pine, while harder woods, such as oak and elm, were used in the construction of the legs and underframe. These pine tops, especially those of some early American tables, were often made from a single piece of wood. With the abundant supply of virgin forest at their disposal, it was not uncommon for the early settlers to find trees of considerable girth, trees that yielded boards between 3 and 4 feet in width.

Like all board material used at that time, the lumber would have been laboriously sawn by hand. The technique employed was known as pit-sawing. The saw used for this was more than 6 feet in length,

Above - GOOD, EASILY ACCESSIBLE STORAGE IS AN ESSENTIAL INGREDIENT IN THE WELL-RUN KITCHEN. THIS LARGE, BUILT-IN WOODEN HUTCH OFFERS EVERYTHING FROM DEEP DRAWERS AND ENCLOSED AND GLAZED CABINETS TO A HANDY THREE-TIER PLATE RACK.

Left - THE SIMPLICITY OF WIDE, BARE FLOORBOARDS, A PLAIN WOODEN BENCH, A BASIC TRESTLE TABLE, AND A LARGE AND USEFUL CUPBOARD CONTRAST STRIKINGLY WITH THE ELEGANT 18TH-CENTURY SASH WINDOWS IN THIS AMERICAN KITCHEN. THE WOVEN RUG AND MATS ADD A WELCOME TOUCH OF COLOR.

and two men were needed to operate it. With the log to be sawn secured lengthwise over a pit dug in the ground (or sometimes supported on a very heavy framework raised above it), one man stood on top of the log and the other below it. Between them, they pushed and pulled the saw progressively through the log. It was hard work, and sweat and sawdust fell freely until the entire log was converted into usable boards. Knowing about and appreciating the toil required in obtaining sawn boards by this method are part of what makes old furniture so very special.

The warmth of wood is an invitation to conviviality, and a wooden table, unadorned with cloth or covers, is the perfect setting for good food. Tables vary enormously in design and regional features, especially in the type of underframe used to make them. Among the earliest are those that developed from a separate board-and-trestle arrangement, which consisted of a pair of shaped trestles linked together with a cross-member tenoned through and secured with wedges. Benches frequently utilize this type of construction, too. Similar, but more lightly made table supports, common in Shaker furniture, are known as "I" trestles. The so-called "joyned," or frame-jointed, table is familiar to us, along with the type with a leg at each corner. There are many variations of this latter type, with either square or lathe-turned legs.

One table design, which originated with the early American settlers, is the sawbuck, or "X"-frame, table. This is a type of trestle arrangement, and when you find one that is well made with cross-lapped joints, you have a very durable table support. In some parts of the country, it is known as the ten-dollar table because its "X" shape is the same as the Roman numeral for the number ten.

Tables designed to extend in size were often of the gate-leg type, a popular design on both sides of the Atlantic. The Pembroke style, which has long side flaps supported on hinged wooden brackets, was also popular. Various small tables were found to be useful both in the kitchen-dining room and elsewhere in the house. Among these were the different designs of occasional table that evolved, as well as what are now generally known as tavern tables. These tavern tables can be found with round, square, and, occasionally, oval tops.

Above, left - MODERN FURNITURE IS SKILLFULLY INTEGRATED INTO A RESTORED AMERICAN KITCHEN. THE HANDMADE PINE CUPBOARDS, DESIGNED TO ACCOMMODATE A MODERN STOVETOP AND OTHER APPLIANCES, BLEND WELL WITH THE ORIGINAL BARE WOODEN FLOORBOARDS. THE TALL STOOL IS MODERN, TOO.

Below, left - THE ADJOINING DINING ROOM IS CLEVERLY SEPARATED FROM THE KITCHEN BY A LOW WOODEN PARTITION, PROVIDING A SEPARATE EATING AREA WHILE STAYING TRUE TO THE OPEN-PLAN STYLE OF MANY EARLY SETTLER HOMES.

Right - THE RUSTIC CHARM OF THIS ROOM LIES IN THE FREEDOM OF ITS COLORFUL CLUTTER AND THE MIXTURE OF PLAIN AND PAINTED WOODEN PIECES.

SEATING SOLUTIONS

An assortment of chairs, as well as benches, can be used to provide seating around a table. Well-used Windsors, in many different styles, can be found made from such woods as ash or yew. The saddled elm seats of older Windsors portray the grain of a hundred years of growth, and their polished patina an additional hundred years of use. Arranged with care in a room, they seem to glow a mellow welcome in the flicker of a log fire or in the candlelight of an intimate evening meal. Fine ladderbacks, English Gimson, or American Shaker – dark-stained or honey-colored natural beech, ash, or hickory – add that authentic touch of rural crafts. With their hand-woven cane or rush seats and simple shapes, these are the first true chairs of the countryside.

Early chair makers chose their wood with particular care, preferring woods like ash and hickory for their resilience, and oak and maple for their strength. Using simple tools – the ax predominantly – wood was split, or cleft, along the grain in order to retain its fibrous strength. It would then be shaped by hand, first with a drawknife and then on simple foot-operated lathes. To make the curved parts, the wood was first steamed and then bent into shape while it was still pliable. The components were then jointed and assembled tight – this, and the juxtaposition of opposing components, constituted the inherent tension that held the finished chair together indefinitely. Many of the chairs made in this way during the 19th century are still in serviceable use today, but good examples are no longer easy to find, so they often fetch a high price in antique shops. Mass-produced reproductions abound, some better than others. However, the best examples are still the ones that have been made by

craftspeople following traditional methods of production. A small but growing number of makers produce chairs in this manner, having studied the old ways of working. Many chair makers work alone, and most create authentic country chairs in a variety of designs, which can then be given either a modern, usually clear, finish, or an antique stained and distressed appearance.

HUTCHES

In large kitchen-dining rooms, a dresser, or hutch, of some type would have held pride of place. The word *dresser* is Norman French in origin, coming from *dressour,* which is the verb to dress, in the sense of to prepare. The hutch of today is a development of the highly ornate, medieval court cupboard, which was primarily used to display the splendor of the wealthy owner's "plate." It is also a close relative of the sideboard of the same and later periods. In the early 17th century, the dresser reappeared again, but this time as a piece of furniture associated more with the country kitchen or dining room than the baronial hall.

At this time, the hutch was little more than a side table on which food was prepared, or dressed, in readiness for cooking or for serving at the dining table. Some were fitted with drawers below the work surface, and most stood on turned legs. A positive step toward the kitchen hutch as we know it today took place in about 1690, when a low backboard was added to the dresser top and, on the wall behind, a row of shelves was attached to serve as a plate rack. The "plate" now was not of gold and silver, however, as in medieval times, but of pewter and earthenware and, later, blue-and-white willow-pattern pottery.

Above - THE LADDERBACK OR SLAT-BACK CHAIR IS A TRADITIONAL DESIGN FOR COUNTRY CHAIRS. THIS PARTICULAR CHAIR WAS MADE FOR A CHILD. LIT BY THE GLOW OF THE LATE AFTERNOON SUN AND USED AS A RESTING PLACE FOR A COLORFUL PUMPKIN, IT MAKES A DELIGHTFUL STILL LIFE.

Right - HUTCHES MIGHT HAVE BEEN DESIGNED PURELY FOR DISPLAY PURPOSES, AND IF, AS HERE, YOU POSSESS A FINE COLLECTION OF COLORFUL GLAZED POTTERY, A HUTCH IS THE PLACE TO PUT IT ON SHOW. NOTE THE DESIRABLE ROUND TAVERN TABLE ON THE RIGHT AND THE PAINTED KNIFE BOX ON THE TABLE.

From these very mixed beginnings, a number of distinct regional styles of hutch emerged – many of them lumped together today, quite incorrectly, under the one general term of "Welsh dresser." Of the several different styles, the one closest to the 18th-century original is that correctly known as the "pot-board dresser." This piece of furniture has the top supporting a plain rack of shelves with shaped side supports and a molded cornice. Below the top are two or more drawers supported underneath by turned legs. These legs are joined together at floor level by a wide, continuous shelf – the pot board. Another type of hutch has its lower section below the drawers fitted

with more shelves and enclosed by doors to form two or three cupboards. A third type has two cupboards and a central opening, or knee hole; while the hutch known as the Irish coop hutch incorporates an enclosed space with a slatted wooden front in which it was the custom to keep laying hens – the warmth indoors encouraged the hens to continue laying eggs during the winter months. Rabbits were also known to have been kept in such hutches in the winter, to keep them warm and as a source of readily available food.

Whatever its type or style, the hutch is a much-used and much-loved piece of furniture. It provides an esthetic as well as a decorative focal point while, at the same time, providing a functional storage and display space in the kitchen or dining room. The Scotsman, John Claudius Loudon, author of *Encyclopaedia of Cottage, Farm and Villa Architecture and Furniture,* published in 1833, says that: ". . . dressers [hutches] are essential to every kitchen, but more especially to the cottager, to whom they serve both as dresser and sideboard. They are generally well made of deal [pine] by local joiners [carpenters] and seldom painted, it being the pride of good housewives, in most parts of England, to keep the boards of which they are composed as white as snow by frequently scouring them with fine sand."

UTENSILS, IMPLEMENTS, AND CONTAINERS

The use of wood in the kitchen-dining room area is not restricted to furniture alone – it was also used extensively for most of the utensils and implements employed in food preparation. With the exception of an iron cooking pot or two and a few metal knives, almost everything else in daily use – spoons, ladles, platters, bowls, rolling pins, and cutting boards – were fashioned from wood, either homemade or bought from local craftspeople. Their makers shared a common knowledge about which wood to use and how to make each particular item.

Before designers had the opportunity to become obsessed with such materials as plastics, aluminum, and stainless steel, wood was also used in a variety of other ways, notably for containers and "smallware" of all descriptions. Smallware is an imprecise term covering such things as boxes, spoon racks, dough troughs, tubs, and buckets. Some of these wooden objects were simply, often crudely, made; others, however, displayed a great deal of innate skill and reveal much about their makers. Examples of smallware include spoons and ladles, which, although almost always strictly utilitarian in purpose – an exception was the love spoon (for more details see page 87) – frequently have such graceful shapes and lines that they are a joy to behold and to touch and use.

Left - CONTAINERS OF ALL KINDS, FOR STORAGE, MIXING, AND SERVING, ARE IMPORTANT PIECES OF EQUIPMENT IN ANY KITCHEN, AND IN THE PAST THESE WERE OFTEN MADE FROM WOOD AND EITHER LEFT PLAIN OR PAINTED. THE SELECTION SHOWN ON THE LEFT REPRESENTS YEARS OF ENJOYABLE COLLECTING BY ONE AMERICAN COOK WITH AN EYE TO THEIR BEAUTY AS WELL AS THEIR USEFULNESS.

Above - AN OVERLADEN STORAGE SHELF HOLDS A VARIETY OF OLD WOODEN CONTAINERS: A LARGE BRIGHT RED BOWL, A FINE OLD COOPERED PAIL, FOUR ROUND BOXES IN DIMINISHING DIAMETERS, AND AN UPTURNED RECTANGULAR DOUGH BOWL PAINTED BLUE.

Containers and vessels for a wide variety of household applications are sometimes ingenious in their construction. Round and oval boxes, for example, created from thin pieces of maple, birch, or cherry wood required special skills to make. Steamed to make the wood pliable, and then bent to make the right shape on formers/forms, these boxes have carefully riveted seams. The best examples of these boxes were fashioned with distinctive and delicately shaped overlapping "fingers," secured with copper rivets at the joint. Decorative but practical, too, the technique of leaving spaces between the fingers allowed the thin, wooden sides to shrink or swell with any changes in humidity, so minimizing the risk of the box's warping or splitting, as was common with straight-jointed boxes. This style of traditional box was adopted and perfected by the various Shaker communities in the United States. These storage boxes were made in a variety of sizes to stack tidily one on top of the other, combining neatness and utility with a religious undertone: piled in this way, the boxes also represent the "stairs to heaven," which every Shaker yearned to climb. The boxes were often painted in earthy colors such as buttermilk yellow, soft brick red, or blueberry. Perhaps more than any other object, they have become symbolic of the Shaker dedication to fine craftsmanship.

Containers such as buckets, tubs, milk churns, and anything else that needed to hold liquids were made by coopers. With great skill, these craftsmen shaped and fitted together the staves from which the vessels were constructed. Held in place by precisely made wooden or metal hoops, the individual staves were so well fitted that, when complete, the container was both watertight and durable. These items now mostly serve a purely decorative function in the modern country-style kitchen. If you want to give old wooden buckets and tubs a more useful life, use them as containers for plants. Always put a drip tray in the bottom and keep the plant in its original pot so that water can drain away.

In modern homes, you can inject something of the country mood into your surroundings through the judicious use of similar wooden objects. Wood is a timeless, sympathetic material, infinitely adaptable, and capable of blending comfortably with most other materials, fabrics, and pottery, be they old or new. Above all, wood is simply a pleasure to live with.

Right - THE RANGE OF UTENSILS USED IN THE KITCHEN IS ENORMOUS, EVEN TODAY. THE EARLIEST IMPLEMENTS WERE ALWAYS MADE OF WOOD, AND EVEN WHEN METAL CAME INTO WIDESPREAD USE FOR FLATWARE AND OTHER KITCHEN UTENSILS, A WOODEN HANDLE WAS OFTEN STILL PREFERRED. SPOONS AND SPATULAS OF ALL SHAPES AND SIZES ARE STILL IN EVERYDAY USE (*Top left*). WOODEN CLOTHESPINS (*Bottom center*) WERE CHEAPLY MADE BY SPLITTING TWIGS AND BINDING THEM WITH A STRIP OF TIN. THE HALF-MOON CUTTERS (*Bottom right*) ARE EXCELLENT FOR FINELY CHOPPING VEGETABLES AND HERBS.

SPOON RACK &
SPOONS

The simple wooden spoon, one of the earliest kitchen implements, is still used today by the modern cook and is, in fact, often recommended when mixing ingredients in nonstick cookware. The surfaces of these containers would soon become abraded by a metal mixing spoon. However, wooden spoons sold in stores today are mere shadows of what they once were. Not only are these modern spoons pretty well standardized and mass-produced, they are also flat and uninteresting, suitable really only for the practical purpose for which they are recommended.

A wooden spoon was once an item of great importance in both town and country households, where it was used not only in the preparation of food but also, together with a pointed knife (forks came on the scene much later), for eating it. Antique examples show a wonderful and truly diverse variety of shapes and sizes – long handles, short handles, some straight and others curved, spoons with large bowls, small bowls, but almost always deep bowls. Spoons in those days were made to hold a generous helping of thick stew, soup or broth, which was how most food was prepared – not the timid, polite quantities favored in countries where a high percentage of the population is at any one time embarking on a diet.

All these spoons were made by hand, and the carving of them was carried out by full-time spoon carvers or by others as a pastime in the long winter evenings. Most spoons were strictly for utilitarian purposes,

but others were highly ornate, even fanciful. These decorated examples were often given by their makers as a token of affection to a sweetheart. Love spoons, as these later came to be called, date back three centuries or more. Originally, it seems, they were intended to be used by the recipient, but as the carving became more and more elaborate, they took on a purely symbolic role. A spoon carved with a single heart indicated "I love you," while an eye meant "I like what I see." To signify mutual love, a spoon would be carved with two bowls, or two spoons would be joined together by a linked chain.

In Wales, particularly, love spoons are still made for the tourist trade, but they have none of the history or the romance of the genuine articles. Antique love spoons are much sought after and collected these days for wall displays in kitchens or breakfast rooms.

Since they were regarded as treasured possessions, spoons (and knives, too) were generally well looked after. While knives were usually stored in specially made boxes, spoons would most often be kept in small, open wooden racks that hung on the wall. Here, they would be conveniently on hand as well as acting as a decorative feature in the kitchen. Sometimes spoon racks were combined with knife boxes, while others might incorporate a compartment for scouring and cleaning materials. The racks themselves ranged from plain and simply made to beautifully carved and painted – perhaps the latter were given as gifts in a similar manner to the ornate love spoons.

Left - ON THE WALL OF THIS TYPICAL COUNTRY KITCHEN HANGS A COLLECTION OF WOODEN SPOONS HOUSED IN A SIMPLE, CUTOUT WOODEN SPOON RACK. THIS HAS BEEN MADE RECENTLY AND GIVEN A TIME-WORN, ANTIQUE APPEARANCE BY DISTRESSING THE PAINTWORK.

Above - SPOONS WERE ONCE REGARDED WITH MORE RESPECT THAN THEY ARE TODAY, AND MUCH CARE AND ATTENTION WENT INTO THEIR MAKING. HIGHLY DECORATED SPOONS WERE GIVEN AS LOVE TOKENS AND WOULD OFTEN BE PROUDLY DISPLAYED IN A SPECIALLY MADE SPOON RACK.

SPOON RACK

ABILITY LEVEL: Novice/ Intermediate

SIZE: 13 x 9 x 5⅝ inches

MATERIALS: Pine, Cherry

CUTTING LIST:
1 front
8 x 6 x ⅜ inches

1 back
8 x 6 x ⅜ inches

2 sides
9 x 5⅝ x ⅜ inches

2 step fronts
8¾ x 1½ x ⅜ inches

3 step tops
9 x 1⅞ x ⅜ inches

See template patterns on page 151 for the back and front pieces.

SPOONS

ABILITY LEVEL: Novice/Intermediate

SIZE: 10 x 2½ x 1½ inches

MATERIALS: Sycamore, Lime, Beech

CUTTING LIST (each spoon):
10 x 2½ x 1½ inches

All measurements are given in inches.

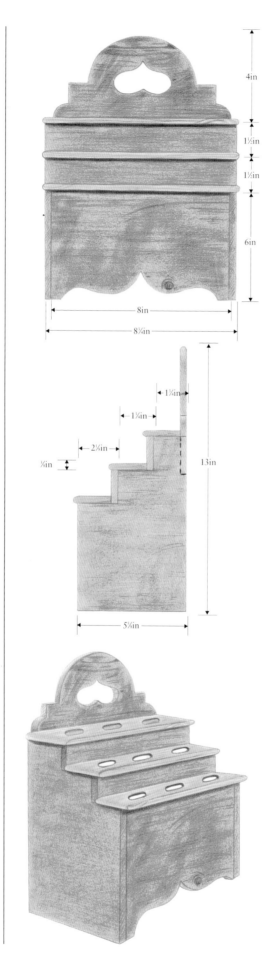

SPOON RACK METHOD:

1. Mark the required pieces and cut them out to the sizes given.

2. On each of the two side pieces, mark out the "step" shaping. Take care when measuring and marking to make sure that the separate pieces fit at the assembly stage.

3. Cut each side piece out to the drawn shape. The sawn edges will later be covered, but it is a good idea to clean them up to encourage a good glued fit of the step fronts and tops.

4. Trace the full-sized template patterns of the back and front pieces (see page 151) and transfer these shapes to the appropriate pieces of wood.

5. Cut these pieces to shape (see page 137 for advice on cutting). Cut the internal shape with a coping saw after first drilling through the wood.

6. Clean off all marks and sand smooth.

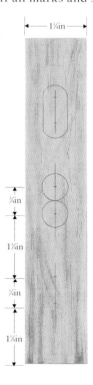

7. To accommodate the spoons, mark the three step top pieces as shown, or figure out and mark any other configuration of holes and slots that you choose.

8. Drill or cut them as required. Drill through into a spare piece of wood to prevent the underside from splintering. Sand back any rough edges.

9. Round over or bevel the front edges and ends of each step top.

10. Check that everything fits together correctly, and in particular, that the two step front pieces fit neatly under the overhang of the step tops.

11. Now clean off all surface marks and pencil lines before assembly.

12. Glue and nail the spoon rack together (see pages 140 and 141 for advice). Begin by assembling the front piece between the two side pieces and then add the back piece.

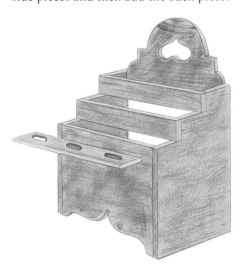

13. Next, put the two step fronts in position and, finally, add the three step tops, beginning at the bottom.

14. Wipe off any surplus glue, set all nail heads below the surface, and fill the indentations. Leave the piece to dry.

15. Clean up and apply a finish of your choice (see pages 146-7).

SPOONS METHOD:

1. Traditionally, wooden spoons were made by splitting a small sycamore log, about 4 inches diameter, into two halves and then roughly chopping the outside shape with a sharp, short-handled ax.

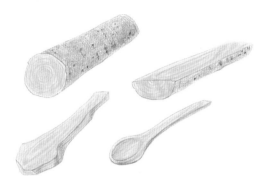

2. After this, the bowl was hollowed out using a special crooked or bent knife. The traditional Welsh carving tool (a *twca cam*) has a short, hooked blade and a straight handle some 18 inches long. Today, hooked knives, often of Swedish origin, are readily obtainable and can be used successfully instead.

3. Final shaping and finishing was accomplished by means of another small knife and a spokeshave.

4. Spoons can also be shaped by sawing and hollowing out using a curved woodcarver's gouge. The most suitable type is the long, bent gouge designed for scooping out concave shapes. A medium size, medium sweep gouge is best; a ¾-inch No. 6 is fine for the job. You must keep the gouge sharp, however (see page 138 for advice).

5. In this method, the bowl is hollowed out first, before the outside is shaped. This allows the work piece to be held safely while the hollowing-out takes place.

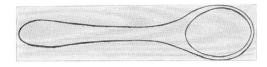

6. Select the material and mark the shape of your spoon; then clamp the piece securely to a workbench, making sure it is in a comfortable working position.

7. Start at the center and work outward. More or less concentrically, start to remove waste wood from the bowl. Use the gouge with a scooping action, going into and out of the material to remove a chip of wood each time. Don't dig in and take care not to go too deep. Aim to get a good finish from a sharp gouge wherever possible.

8. Remove from the clamp and saw the outside to shape (see page 137 for advice).

9. Complete the shaping of the outside by whittling with a knife, or use a rasp and file. Finish off with fine sandpaper for a smooth appearance, if required. Tool marks shaped with a sharp knife can add character if they are left showing.

10. Don't apply any finish. After use, clean spoons by washing and occasional scouring. Never leave a wooden spoon soaking in water for any length of time.

11. Try making some of the alternative shapes shown in the opening photograph. Sometimes handles were embellished with simple, carved decoration and this could be added if you wish.

SCOOPS & LADLES

The name "scoop" derives from the old Dutch word *schope* and is also related to the Middle High German *scephan*, which means to ladle. While the words scoop and ladle are often used synonymously, scoops generally have short handles and are used for such dry goods as flour, legumes, and herbs, while ladles usually have long handles and are intended mainly for use with liquids.

Another distinction between the two is that scoops tend to be broader and flatter than ladles, but both – made of wood – were in common, everyday use in the households, and especially the kitchens, of countless generations of people before the introduction of plastics and stainless steel. There, they played an important part in both the preparation and serving of food and drink, often being used for mixing and measuring – along with spoons – as well as for transferring ingredients from one container or cooking vessel to another. They were also found in the farm dairy, for milk, and for butter and cheese making, a special perforated scoop was used to skim cream from the whey.

It is not unusual to find ladles with spouts, like pitchers, to help direct the flow of the liquid more accurately, and often they have hooked handles so that they can be hung up out of the way or conveniently hooked over the side of the container they are being used in. The short-handled ladle shown in the

project is known as a churn ladle. Note the large hooked handle, which not only allows it to be hung up, but also forms a steady support when the ladle is placed down, full of milk, on a flat surface. Along with other wooden utensils and implements, such ladles were in regular use in the dairies well into the 20th century.

All types and designs of ladles and scoops were made, shaped, and carved by hand by local craftspeople or by members of the household. When sycamore was available, it was the preferred material to use because it does not impart any smell or taste. Although primarily utilitarian in purpose, some scoops and ladles were decorated with carvings, especially on their handles, while others were made from exotic imported woods. Ladles, or dippers, with quite small bowls – they were also known as punch or cordial ladles – were often quite intricately made and were kept especially for serving these beverages on formal occasions.

Wooden ladles and scoops are among the most collected of kitchen memorabilia, and their popularity is almost certainly attributable to the fact that so much in the way of kitchenware these days is either made from metal or plastic. Wooden utensils are so much more simple and utilitarian compared to many of their modern counterparts, and their appearance, well used and well worn, gives them considerable character and charm.

Above - AN 18TH-CENTURY DINING ROOM SIDEBOARD PROVIDES THE IDEAL LOCATION TO DISPLAY A COLLECTION OF 18TH- AND 19TH-CENTURY KITCHEN-WARE. AMONG THEM ARE TWO WELL-USED WOODEN SCOOPS, A LONG-HANDLED LADLE, AND TWO HIGHLY DECORATIVE WOODEN BUTTER MOLDS.

Right - WHETHER OLD OR NEW, WOODEN SPOONS AND SCOOPS – AND ALL MANNER OF OTHER DOMESTIC UTENSILS, TOO – SERVE BOTH A PRACTICAL AND A DECORATIVE PURPOSE IN TODAY'S KITCHEN. THEY ARE IMMENSELY SATISFYING TO HANDLE, AND SCOOPS IN PARTICULAR MAKE EXCELLENT SERVERS.

ABILITY LEVEL: Novice/Intermediate

SIZE: 12 x 6 x 3 inches

MATERIALS: Sycamore, Beech, Lime

CUTTING LIST:
(**Flour scoop**) 10 x 5 x 2½ inches

(**Churn ladle**) 10 x 6 x 4 inches

(**Ladle with spout**) 13 x 5 x 3 inches

All measurements are given in inches.

METHOD:

1. Working in the traditional way, a small, often unseasoned log would be selected. This would be split in two and a scoop or ladle chopped out and shaped from each half using a short-handled, very sharp ax.

2. The bowl's inner shape was then roughly hollowed out using a variety of tools, including curved gouges, hooked knives, or – for larger pieces of wood – a small hand adze. The bowl of the scoop or ladle would be completed with a rounded carving gouge or, in some areas, a special hooked knife. A curved woodcarver's gouge, of the type known as a long bent gouge, is suitable for this job. The final shaping and finishing of the outside was done with either a short-bladed knife or a drawknife or spokeshave.

3. Early makers were able to use these tools with great skill and little danger to themselves. The novice is strongly advised, however, to employ safer methods of working, at least to begin with.

4. More modern methods of working include using sawn pieces of wood, which are marked out in outline and then partially hand or band sawn to the required outside shape. The inside shape of the bowl is produced by carving with the piece safely clamped to the bench.

FLOUR SCOOP (1-inch squares)

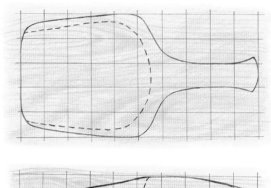

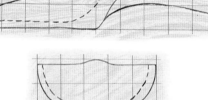

5. To make the flour scoop, mark out the shape on the piece of wood by enlarging and using the pattern produced here. First, mark out and saw only to the plan shape. If you are hand sawing, make sure that the piece is held securely in a vise.

6. With the piece clamped by the handle portion, hollow out the concave scoop with a carving gouge. Begin at the front (open) end of the scoop and work gradually backward in stages, biting deeper into the wood each time. Finish with the gouge using lighter and longer strokes to leave the wood as smooth as you can.

7. When you are satisfied with the inside shape and surface, mark the side view and remove the waste wood down to the lines you have drawn (mainly under the handle). Sawing by hand is best and safest. Complete the outside shape with a spokeshave or use a rasp and file. Next, shape the handle and bring the front to a firm edge.

8. Finish the flour scoop by sanding the wood until it is smooth.

CHURN LADLE (1-inch squares)

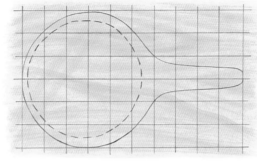

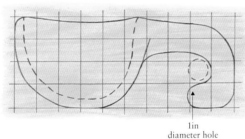

1in
diameter hole

9. Because of the generous shape of the churn ladle, you will need a substantial piece of wood. As before, mark out its plan and side views, but do not saw it to shape until after the bowl has been hollowed out.

Clamp the piece to the bench and, using a carver's gouge, begin at the center and work outward, more or less concentrically, to

remove waste wood from the bowl. Use the gouge with a scooping action, in conjunction with a mallet if it helps you. Don't let the gouge dig in.

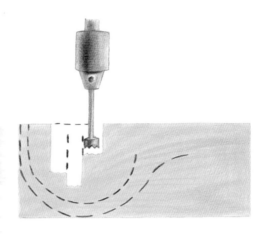

10. An alternative is to remove some of the waste wood by drilling it out. Finish the shaping with a gouge or hooked knife.

11. When the bowl is satisfactory, saw to the drawn plan shape, then draw in the side view. Begin the outside shaping first by drilling through to form the inside of the hooked handle, as shown. Then hand saw the waste wood away to the drawn lines.

12. Using tools of your choice, shape the outside of the bowl and handle. Keep the hook of the handle fairly substantial so that it does not break across the end grain, and keep its lower edge flat so that it make a good support when the ladle is at rest. Finish by sanding it smooth.

LADLE WITH SPOUT (1-inch squares)

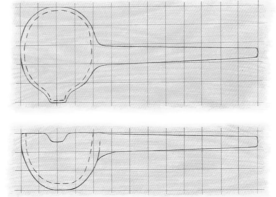

13. The ladle with the pouring spout has a shallower bowl and a long, round handle. Making this safely is best done by holding

the wood in a vise and working on the bowl first. More experienced woodworkers may prefer to work in the traditional way, whittling with a knife or gouge while holding the wood in the hand.

14. With the plan and side views drawn in, and the piece clamped to the bench, begin by hollowing out the bowl as described for the churn ladle (see step 9). Take care in shaping the spout portion and leave it a little oversize at this stage.

15. When you are happy with the shape of the bowl, saw away the waste wood to the drawn plan and side views. Keep the handle full and square at this stage and start shaping the outside of the bowl. Pay particular attention to the shape of the spout to ensure that it pours properly.

16. Finally, form the round handle using a knife, spokeshave or rasp. Flare the handle out slightly where it joins the bowl to give it extra strength. Finish by sanding it smooth.

17. Like spoons and cutting boards (see pages 89 and 96), scoops and ladles may be left untreated and kept clean by washing and scrubbing them. Never leave them soaking in water for hours at a time.

18. Good work is characterized by good proportions and bowl edges that are strong but not too thick. Final shaping with sharp cutting tools gives a more pleasing texture than a too-smooth finish obtained by sanding.

CUTTING
BOARDS

One of the most useful, and certainly one of the most often used, items in the kitchen has always been the traditional wooden cutting board. In addition to having pride of place on the table when slicing bread or cheese, cutting boards are invaluable accessories in the preparation of all manner of vegetables, meat, and fish. Cutting boards feature prominently not only in the kitchens of country-style homes, but also in large, up-to-the-minute modern domestic and commercial kitchens. Even in today's world of ready-prepared convenience foods and sliced bread, they still retain their usefulness – and they look good, too.

As the companion to the good cook's most precious tool of the trade – a sharp, well-balanced knife – a cutting board makes an ideal surface for cutting, slicing, and chopping, all of which, until the end of the 19th century, had to be done by hand. All kinds of implements were made to complement the cutting boards of the day; not just knives, but also various types of blades. Some cutting tools were cast in one piece with iron handles; others had separate blades mounted on wooden handles. Curved blades were designed mostly for use in round bowls and mortars; tools with straight or slightly curved blades were used with flat boards. Implements with curved blades often had a handle at each end of the blade, and some had multiple blades to speed the work. The advantage of using a wooden surface is that it does not blunt the knife blade as quickly as some other materials, and, contrary to some modern

ideas, if wood is properly cleaned after use, it is not an unhygienic work surface.

Cutting boards are available in all shapes and sizes. Many are simply plain, rectangular boards, either made from a single piece of wood or pieces jointed together. Others have handles and a means by which they can be hung up when not in use. When kneading bread dough and for rolling out pastry (with a wooden rolling pin), especially large boards are used; these often doubled as the lid to the dough bin or trough. This held the prepared dough near the warmth of the fire to rise before being baked. For slicing and serving bread or cake at the table, circular and sometimes decoratively carved boards were once, and still are, very popular.

The wood used for cutting boards, or any other wooden objects that come into contact with food, is important. It must be close grained and stable, and it must not impart any taste or have any odor. It also needs to be clean-looking and able to be kept properly clean. Sycamore meets these criteria best, with beech and maple close contenders. Pine is often used because of its low cost. However, it is too soft and does not wear well with use. Ideally, a cutting board should be left untreated and should be cleaned after every use with a clean, damp cloth or brush. If the board has been used for preparing fish or meat, scrub it thoroughly with soap and hot water, rinse off, and leave to dry. In the past, cutting boards were kept clean by scouring them regularly with wet sand.

Left - KITCHEN OBJECTS SUCH AS CUTTING BOARDS, IN ADDITION TO SERVING A PRACTICAL FUNCTION IN MANY CULINARY PROCESSES, ARE UNDENIABLY DECORATIVE. THEIR WELL-USED SIMPLICITY LENDS CHARACTER TO THE COTTAGE KITCHEN IN TOWN AND COUNTRY ALIKE.

Above - CUTTING BOARDS LEND THEMSELVES TO AN INFINITE VARIETY OF DESIGNS, FROM THE PLAIN AND PRACTICAL TO THE EQUALLY USEFUL BUT WHIMSICAL. IT IS POSSIBLE TO COME BY PAIRS OF ANIMAL-SHAPED CUTTING BOARDS, AND THEY ADD AN EXTRA HOMEY, RUSTIC TOUCH TO A COUNTRY-STYLE HUTCH.

ABILITY LEVEL: Novice/Intermediate

SIZE: 12 x 10 x 1 inches

MATERIALS: Sycamore, Beech, Maple, Pine

CUTTING LIST:
(**Rectangular board**) 12 x 10 x 1 inches

(**Handled board**) 14 x 8 x 1 inches

(**Circular board**) 10 x 10 x 1 inches

See template patterns on pages 150-1 for handle of handled board, and pattern on circular board

All measurements are given in inches.

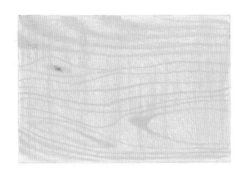

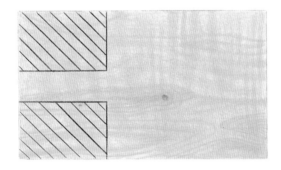

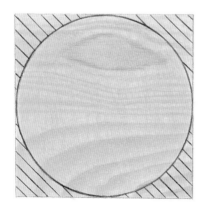

METHOD:

1. Select well-seasoned material wide enough across the grain to match, or at least approximate, the dimensions given.

2. Where this is not possible, you can make boards up out of narrower pieces edge-joined together (see page 141 for advice on edge joining). Make sure you use a good-quality waterproof adhesive.

3. Plane or sand both surfaces clean and perfectly flat.

4. Where required, draw the outline of the shape directly onto the wood and cut it to shape using any safe method (see page 137 for advice on cutting). Always cut on the outside (the waste side) of the drawn line.

5. The rectangular board is easily marked out using a set square and ruler. The handle of the handled board is marked out and cut to the pattern given on page 150. The circular board is marked out by using a pair of compasses.

6. Clean up the sawn edge surfaces by planing any long straight edges, taking care with the end grain. Use a suitable file or other abrasive tool to clean up curved edges and to get into any awkward corners. Or use a spokeshave. Round over or chamfer the edges so that they are not sharp. Finish off with fine sandpaper.

7. The rectangular cutting board is now complete (see also step 10).

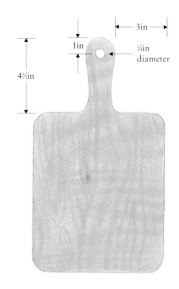

8. If you wish to hang the handled board, drill a ¼-inch hole through the handle and thread a cord for hanging.

9. The circular board has one flat surface decorated with carving. To help you reproduce this design, a pattern is given on page 151. You can trace this and transfer it to your board or devise a pattern of your own design. Or you can leave the board plain and simply round its edges over.

10. For regular use, the boards should be left untreated with no surface finish at all. Keep them clean by regularly wiping them with a damp cloth and an occasional scrub in water. Use hot water and soap to clean boards on which meat or fish have been prepared. If a finished surface is required, apply several coats of vegetable oil to the wood.

Right - THE RUGGEDNESS OF A WELL-USED BUTCHER'S CHOPPING BLOCK ON A COUNTERTOP AND THE SCRUBBED SURFACES OF THE CUTTING BOARDS DISPLAYED BELOW PROVIDE A STRONG CONTRAST OF TEXTURE WITH THE SMOOTH, POLISHED, DOUBLE-BOW WINDSOR CHAIR IN THIS ENGLISH KITCHEN.

Wall-mounted boxes for storing all manner of domestic odds and ends were once very common. Ranks of simple open shelving, designed to help keep work surfaces clear of clutter and for displaying ornaments and prized family possessions, were supplemented in many homes by small cupboards of the type shown below. Cupboards such as these could be found in any room of the house. In the kitchen, one could be used for cooking utensils or for canned or packaged foods and spices. In a bathroom, a cupboard much like this makes an ideal medicine cabinet, while in a family room, wall cupboards could be used for housing books, important family papers and documents, or as a liquor cabinet. A lock could easily be put on, especially if medicines or alcohol were to be kept inside. Cupboards used for storing food are often found with pierced fronts, or with front panels made of perforated tinplate, to allow fresh air to circulate inside to keep food cool and the flies out. Early descriptive names for food cupboards include "meat safe" and "pie safe."

The term wall cupboard obviously describes a container that is designed to be hung on a wall, and for this reason they are also often described as hanging cupboards. If they are further described as being enclosed, they also had a door – a seemingly unnecessary adjunct now, since in modern parlance many pieces of wooden furniture with doors can generally be described as

cupboards. But this was not always so. Primarily, the cupboard or, more correctly, the *cup-board* or *cup-borde,* was a medieval contrivance, which consisted of a supported board or plank of wood on which drinking vessels were placed during a meal. This use was to give rise to the parallel evolution of the sideboard and the hutch.

Another ancient name, now mainly used, or misused, by furniture historians and antique dealers is, in fact, more closely related to the modern concept of the cupboard. This is the *aumbry* or *armoire,* which is a box-like structure with shelves and, more important, doors. The earliest form of armoire was made to fit into a niche cut into the fabric of the wall, but by the late Middle Ages, freestanding versions were commonplace. These were used for many different purposes, both secular and sacred. The livery cupboard, for example, had holes pierced in the doors for ventilation and was used for storing food for the servants of great houses (hence the term "liveried servant.") The word armoire is still used to describe a form of freestanding cabinet for storing clothes.

The provision of an enclosed cupboard designed for storing food has continued uninterrupted to the present time, and is an essential piece of furniture in any kitchen. The cupboard described here, although rather elaborate for a country-style piece, is based on a cupboard said to have been made in Pennsylvania in about 1750.

Left - THE ORGANIZED COOK BELIEVES THAT THERE IS "A PLACE FOR EVERYTHING AND EVERYTHING IN ITS PLACE," AND THAT THERE CAN NEVER BE TOO MANY CUPBOARDS AND DRAWERS IN THE KITCHEN. THE SIMPLE DESIGN OF THIS WALL-HUNG CUPBOARD REVEALS ITS COUNTRY ROOTS.

Above - WITH ITS PAINTED, TIME-WORN APPEARANCE, THIS FINELY WORKED CABINET WOULD FIND A PLACE IN ANY FARM OR COTTAGE KITCHEN DESPITE SUCH ELEGANT DETAILS AS THE CORNICED TOP MOLDING AND PANELED DOOR – NOT FEATURES COMMON TO MANY TRUE COUNTRY-MADE CUPBOARDS.

ABILITY LEVEL: Experienced

SIZE: 27 x 20 x 9 inches

MATERIALS: Pine

CUTTING LIST:
CARCASS
2 sides
26 x 7 x ¾ inches
1 top
18¼ x 7 x ¾ inches

1 bottom
18¼ x 7 x ¾ inches

1 middle shelf
18¼ x 6¾ x ¾ inches

1 back
26 x 19 x ⅜ inches

FACE FRAME (front)
2 stiles
26 x 3 x ¾ inches

2 rails
16 x 3 x ¾ inches

1 mid rail
16 x 3 x ¾ inches

DOOR
2 stiles
15 x 3 x ¾ inches

2 rails
10 x 3 x ¾ inches

1 panel
10 x 8 x ½ inches

DRAWER
1 front
13 x 3 x ½ inches

2 sides
7 x 3 x ½ inches

1 back
13 x 2½ x ½ inches

1 onset front
13½ x 3½ x ½ inches

1 bottom
12 x 7 x ¼ inches

4 guides
7 x ½ x ½ inches

2 supports
7 x 5½ x ½ inches

CORNICE
1 top rail
21 x 3 x ¾ inches

2 side rails
9 x 3 x ¾ inches

molding
approx 9ft of ¾ x ¾ inches

All measurements are given in inches.

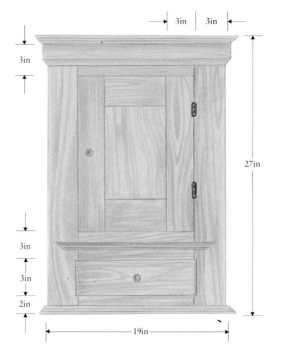

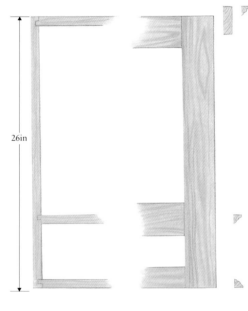

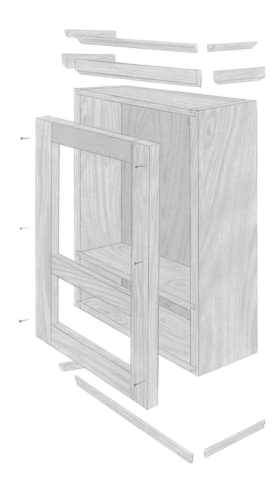

METHOD:

1. Select materials and cut all parts to size. Take care to cut all ends squarely and accurately (see page 137 for advice). Keep all related parts together, for example drawer parts, carcass parts, etc.

2. Begin by planing and then edge-gluing all pieces needed to make wider boards, if necessary.

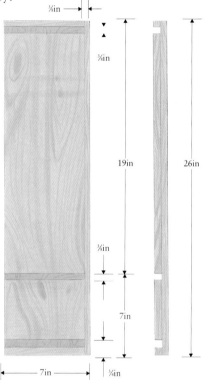

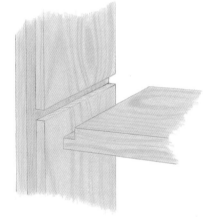

3. Construct the carcass first. Mark and cut out the through dadoes, ¼ inch deep, in the side pieces to accommodate the top, middle, and bottom shelves. Then cut a ⅜-inch rabbet for the back (see page 142 for advice on rabbets).

4. Test fit without using glue, to check that everything fits and is square. Disassemble and clean off any surface marks.

5. Apply glue and assemble the carcass. Again, check that it is square and hold it together with clamps until it is dry.

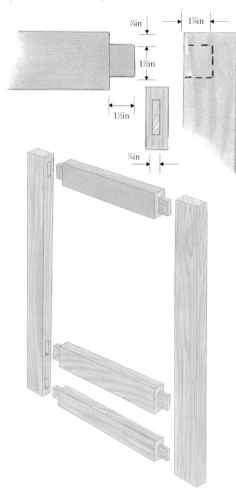

6. Make the front face frame using mortises and tenons (see page 144 for advice on making these joints). Check the lengths of the components. The frame can be slightly larger than the carcass to allow for planing to a flush fit later.

7. Mark and cut out the mortises into each of the stiles, and mark and cut the tenons on each end of the rails. Since the stiles and rails are ¾ inch thick, the mortises and tenons will be ¼ inch.

8. Check that each joint fits well. Then test fit without glue, and check that the frame is square. Disassemble and clean off any surface marks.

9. Apply glue and assemble the front face frame. Hold it with clamps and check that it has not twisted out of square.

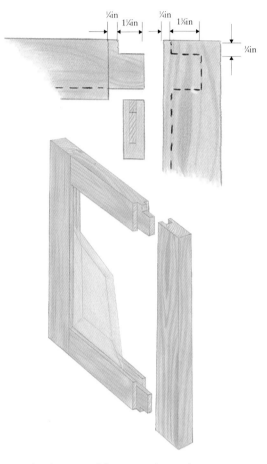

10. The door is of frame and panel construction and has haunched mortise and tenon joints. This, too, should be slightly oversized so that it can be planed to a good fit within the door opening.

11. Cut a ¼-inch wide, ¼-inch deep groove along the inside edge of all four door frame pieces (see page 142 for advice on grooves) to accommodate the panel.

12. Mark and cut out the mortises into both stiles.

13. Mark and cut out the haunched tenons on each end of the rails. The haunch is trimmed to fit and fill the exposed ends of the grooves made in the stiles (see page 142 for grooving and making joints).

14. Test fit each joint and then assemble the door frame, without using glue, to check that it is square.

15. While the door frame is assembled, measure the opening for the door panel. Add ⅜ inch to both the length and the width (to fit into the frame groove). Now disassemble the door frame.

16. Cut the door panel to the precise dimensions determined in step 15. Plane a long bevel all around the panel, as shown, and test fit it in the door frame groove.

17. Assemble the door frame and panel, without using glue, bevel facing outward. Check for square and then disassemble and clean off any surface marks.

18. Glue and assemble the door, but do not glue in the panel. Hold the frame together with clamps and check for square.

19. Attach the front face frame to the carcass by gluing and nailing. Set the nail heads below the surface and fill the indentations. Plane off the frame overlap.

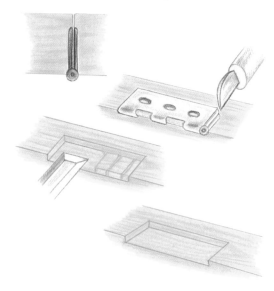

20. Try the door for size in the opening and then trim it to a tight fit. Mark the position of the hinges and chisel out the hinge housings. Test fit and hang the door.

21. To simplify the making of the drawer, through dovetail joints have been used (see page 143 for advice on joints). The onset, or lipped false front, conceals the joints at the front and also eliminates the need for any drawer stops.

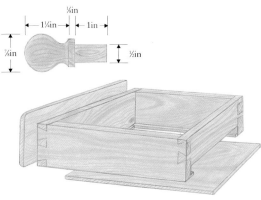

22. Begin by making the drawer front fit the opening. Cut the back to the same length as the front, and the side pieces the same width as the front. Check that the ends are square and mark adjoining parts.

23. Now mark and cut out the dovetail "tails" on the drawer side pieces (see page 143 for advice).

24. Mark out the dovetail "sockets" using the "tails" cut in step 23 as a template.

25. Cut the dovetail "sockets" (see page 143 for advice) and test fit each joint, but avoid handling them too often.

26. Assemble the drawer parts, without using glue, and check for squareness. Disassemble the drawer and clean off any surface marks.

27. Apply glue and assemble the drawer. Clamp it together and check again for squareness. When dry, clean off surplus glue in the joint areas.

28. Fit the drawer bottom, with the grain running from side to side, on slips of wood at the sides and front. Pin it where it passes and overhangs the back. Do not use glue.

29. Glue and nail the onset false front into position, with an equal overhang all around. Set the nail holes below the surface and fill the indentations with woodfiller or a mixture of glue and sawdust. When the glue is thoroughly dry, round over the overhanging front edges.

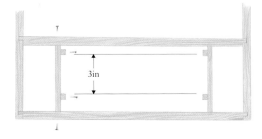

30. The drawer runs between supports and simple guides, fitted as shown.

31. Cut the cornice pieces to length and miter their mating ends. On the lower edges of each piece, plane a ½-inch bevel.

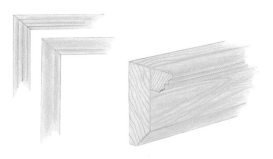

32. Test fit and then glue and nail the cornice into place.

33. Miter and test fit the top and bottom moldings. Glue and pin them into position when you are satisfied. Apply the center molding.

34. Cut the back to size and pin it into its rabbet.

35. Make or buy matching knobs for the door and drawer. Drill tight holes for these and glue them into place.

36. The finish on the original cupboard is flat blue paint applied over layers of earlier paint. See pages 146-7 for ways of achieving a similar antique paint finish.

Right - WALL-HUNG CUPBOARDS COME IN ALL SHAPES AND SIZES, AND VARY FROM THE MOST ELABORATE TO THOSE OF SIMPLE CONSTRUCTION. THIS LONG, NARROW CUPBOARD HAS A PLAIN BOARDED DOOR OF PAINTED PINE AND AN UNUSUAL ROOF-LIKE, ARCHED TOP.

Bedrooms & Bathrooms

BEDROOMS

There is little to match the comfortable intimacy of a country cottage bedroom. Old pine furniture – original or stripped and rewaxed or repainted in earth shades – or the rich patina of polished oak, cherry, or beech, blend beautifully with colored textiles and the sprig patterns of country bedroom wallpaper, bed linen, and draperies.

The bedroom as we think of it today, however, did not really exist until about the beginning of the 18th century. Cottage bedrooms (created in the free space beneath the eaves of the roof) were small and dark and furnished with little more than a bed and bedside chair. In the "big" houses, while the family slept in quite large rooms, their servants slept in attic rooms, which were slightly more spacious than the cottage attic, and often had a dormer window as well to admit some light. These two factors, and a few extra bits of furniture, often discarded from other parts of the house, allowed for more creativity. Thus, much of the inspiration for today's image of the country bedroom comes not from the humble cottage, but from the wealthier household, since more of these examples have survived.

BEDS

The bed – the focal point of any bedroom – can be a simple wooden bedstead, a bare box bed, or perhaps an old trundle or truckle bed. These beds had wheels and were originally kept tucked away under a larger bed in the bedrooms of the better-off, and they would be wheeled (trundled) out when required for the use of a servant or a child. The so-called sleigh bed – a Scandinavian development of the box bed – injects a touch of the exotic into the country theme while, by way of a contrast, the stark austerity and utilitarianism of the Adirondack-style "twig" bed gives a true rustic feel to the cottage bedroom. Beds with headboards lend themselves to restrained decoration, such as carving, piercing, or stenciling. Your tastes might be for a more ornate style of bed, with lathe-turned posts built in the Pennsylvania style. Or you may prefer a simple four-poster.

No matter how plain, grand, or rustic your choice of bed, there is no need to compromise on comfort. Any style of country bed can, of course, be fitted with a modern mattress, appropriately concealed with traditional bedcovers, linen sheets, embroidered pillowcases, and perhaps a colorful hand-crafted quilt.

Above, left - MADE IN MASSACHUSETTS AROUND 1820, THIS BED IS A FINE EXAMPLE OF THE COLONIAL FOUR-POSTER-STYLE. THE CORNER POSTS ARE LATHE-TURNED.

Below, left - A LATHE-TURNED AND RAIL BED, THREE-DRAWER CHEST, AND HANGING SHELF MAKE UP THE THREE KEY ELEMENTS IN THIS COTTAGE BEDROOM.

Left - RESPLENDENT IN A 19TH-CENTURY QUILT, THE ADIRONDACK-STYLE TWIG BED GIVES THIS BEDROOM AN INVITING COUNTRY COMFORTABLENESS.

STORAGE

Furniture for storage is an important consideration in the bedroom. Shelves can serve both a decorative and a practical role, and the hanging shelves characteristic of the Shaker style suit these particular requirements well. The traditional chest and blanket box, which was once used to store everything from personal clothing to clean bed linen, makes a tremendous contribution to the country-cottage look of a room, especially when placed at the foot of a bed. Pine is a popular choice for a blanket box, but you can use other woods, too, especially if they are to be finished with clear varnish to allow the wood grain to show through. Less well figured woods can be plainly painted or decorated in the manner of Pennsylvania dower chests.

Storage furniture in the country house is rarely restricted to use in any one room, and plain chests of drawers, as well as more elaborate pieces with shelves or closed cupboards fitted above, find a place in the bedroom as elsewhere. These "children of the chest" began life when frame and panel construction allowed for a front opening drawer to be fitted in the bottom of the chest. The obvious advantage of the drawer over the box soon led to the development of what we now know as the chest of drawers, in which the entire framework is filled with drawers. Further changes saw these chests of drawers become higher and contain even more drawers, and so the "tallboy" came into being.

From there they evolved into a variety of styles. Those made in the country style are generally of solid construction or are framed and paneled in pine, oak, or cherry. Chests of drawers are usually named for the number of drawers they contain – three, four, and five being the most common numbers.

Purpose-built dressers, complete with pivoting mirrors, are a comparatively modern development in bedroom furniture, and most would be out of place in the country-style bedroom. Instead, consider a small table with a separate, freestanding mirror, or one attached to a wall above it, as a more suitable option. As an alternative, a wooden washstand, typically with a marble top, and complete with a matching porcelain bowl and pitcher might be the perfect design solution for a country-style bedroom.

Left - FURNITURE FROM WIDELY DIFFERENT CULTURES AND REGIONS OFTEN WORKS WELL TOGETHER IN COUNTRY-STYLE INTERIORS. THE BLUE PAINTED CUPBOARD FROM MEXICO PAIRED WITH A RED STOOL FROM JAMAICA BRING A SPLASH OF COLOR TO THIS NEW ENGLAND BEDROOM.

Above, right - AN OLD CHEST OF DRAWERS ALSO SERVES AS A SURFACE FOR A DECORATIVE DISPLAY – SUCH INFORMAL STILL LIFES EPITOMIZE THE COUNTRY STYLE.

Below, right - TRUE TO THE COTTAGE BEDROOM OF OLD, A SMALL TABLE IS USED AS A FORM OF DRESSER INSTEAD OF A PURPOSE-BUILT MODEL.

CLOSETS

Clothes cupboards or "wardrobes" may first have been used in churches as places in which to hang rich vestments and other religious robes. It was not until the 19th century that they came into general use in the home. Before this time, the custom had been to keep clothes folded in chests of drawers rather than to have them hanging up. Where clothes were hung, it was usually in a curtained-off alcove or perhaps in a built-in closet. In medieval times, clothes were sometimes draped or hung from a form of pegboard, not dissimilar in style to the later Shaker pegboard, which was fixed to the wall, although clothes were mainly stored away in large chests.

Freestanding armoires are often large items of furniture, and although you might be able to squeeze one into a small bedroom, its proportions may prove overpowering in such a limited space. Because of this, it is probably better to leave the armoire outside in the hall, as was frequently done in the past. Armoires come in many different sizes, however, so if you persevere you may find one of the right size for your bedroom.

North European and Scandinavian country armoires were often decoratively painted in rich earth colors, with hand-painted or stenciled motifs featuring flowers and foliage. Others were distinguished by heavy moldings and boldly executed carving. Such peasant art, imported into America along with the new settlers, forms the basis for the development of various regional styles seen today.

Above & Right - THE ARMOIRE ABOVE IS FROM FRANCE, AND NOW STANDS IN ALL ITS CARVED SPLENDOR IN A CONNECTICUT HOME. THE EXAMPLE ON THE RIGHT IS LATE 18TH CENTURY, FROM SOUTHERN GERMANY. ITS RICHLY PAINTED MOTIFS ARE REMINISCENT OF PENNSYLVANIAN WORK OF THE SAME PERIOD.

CHILDREN'S BEDROOMS

Early inventories occasionally refer to items of children's furniture, such as cradles, chairs, baby walkers, and similar objects. Numerous 17th-century pieces especially made for use by children, including diminutive beds, have survived to the present day. More often than not, these items of furniture would have been used in shared rooms, since separate bedrooms for younger members of the family were rare until well into the 18th century.

The earliest separate accommodation was the nursery, where children, at least those of the well-to-do, were kept day and night in the care of nurses and nannies. Children were dressed like adults and, even at play, they were being prepared for adulthood – at a time when the horse was the principal means of transportation, the nursery rocking horse was not merely a toy. (Most toys in the past were made of wood, and early wooden toys have become extremely collectible and much sought-after today.) In a similar way, with a few exceptions – such as the cradle – children's furniture was usually designed as scaled-down versions of adult pieces of the period. Even four-poster beds and chairs were made in children's sizes.

This purpose-made and permanent type of nursery furniture probably reached the peak of its popularity in middle-class families during the late 19th century and just into the 20th, when large families were very much the norm. By this time, however, a change in attitude in the way children were brought up was beginning to have an effect on the running of the nursery and on the provision and furnishings of rooms for young people in general.

Nowadays, the nursery is no longer a permanent arrangement. It is used mainly for sleeping purposes only during the first few years of the child's life, and it is considered a bedroom designed to change as the child grows and its needs change.

For the very young child, the cradle has withstood the test of time and remains popular today. In use for centuries, cradles have varied from the earliest woven type to the Gothic swinging crib. The more common type of rocking cradle, like the one described in the project on pages 120-3, has been in use since about the beginning of the 17th century. Examples were found in the cottages of the poorest as well as in the wealthiest of homes.

The earliest cradles were intended to accommodate the needs of babies up until about their third or fourth year. After this age, the child would graduate to a small-sized bed, or crib. "Crib" was the name originally given to small beds with guard rails. Known since Chippendale's time in the mid-18th century, cribs had hinged sides, but now sides that slide up and down are preferred.

For the older child who has outgrown the nursery, the trundle or truckle beds described earlier (see page 106) were convenient and were frequently found in use in children's bedrooms, especially in rural areas. Where space was tight, built-in beds were also quite common; they can incorporate valuable storage space beneath them. Originally rather like bunks on board ships, they have developed into the modern, and very popular, two-tier bunk bed – a design that can solve the problem of making the best use of small-sized bedrooms as the family increases.

Toy boxes remain popular and are used by children for many years. They make convenient storage areas, too, allowing free space on the floor for play. Child-sized chairs and a tables may also be useful for certain games and activities.

As an alternative to new or custom-made furniture, you may prefer to use secondhand pieces, repainted in clean, country colors, or given a protective coat of clear lacquer. But beware of splinters in well-used wooden furniture, especially if it is made from plywood.

Below Left - COZY AS A SHIP'S BUNK, THIS CHILD'S BED, LOCATED UNDER THE EAVES OF A FARMHOUSE IN SUFFOLK, ENGLAND, IS CONSTRUCTED IN PINE TO MATCH THE WALL AND SLOPING CEILING ABOVE. DRAWERS UNDER THE BED AND PEGS ABOVE TAKE CARE OF STORAGE MATTERS.

Left, above & Above - SIMPLE WOODEN TOYS ARE CHARMINGLY EVOCATIVE OF COUNTRY CHILDHOOD DAYS. THESE WELL-LOVED SPECIMENS (LEFT, ABOVE) HAVE CLEARLY GIVEN YEARS OF PLEASURE. THE UNUSED KNIFE BOX (ABOVE) HAS TAKEN ON A NEW LEASE ON LIFE AS A PLACE TO KEEP HOMEMADE RAG DOLLS.

BATHROOMS

If the notion of a country-style bathroom conjures up thoughts of outhouses, cold floors, chipped enamel, and noisy, temperamental plumbing, don't despair. There are ways of combining 20th-century convenience with 19th-century charm. Although the bathroom is often one of the more neglected rooms of the house, it really is the place where you can give your creative instincts free rein. And if your bathroom has to accommodate such mundane things as, say, a hot water heater, it can be built into an attractive wooden cabinet with extra shelves and storage space included.

THE USE OF WOOD

Unless your bathroom is a large room, it will probably contain very little in the way of furniture. Typically, you may find a wall cabinet for medicine and toiletries, a few open shelves for storage, and a stool. To introduce a flavor of country style, you could start by using wood for features such as wall paneling and accessories.

Wood paneling – either floor-to-ceiling or just halfway up – immediately injects a country-style atmosphere into a bathroom. Wood paneling was first used to cover rough stone and brick walls and, incidentally, it provides a reasonable degree of insulation, too, substantially reducing condensation levels, especially in homes where the bathroom is on an exterior wall of the house.

It is common today for wood paneling to be extended to include the "boxing-in" of the bathtub itself. This modern innovation serves the additional function of concealing the plumbing – not usually the most attractive of bathroom features. Inexpensive tongue-and-groove boards made of pine can be used successfully for this job. All bathroom woodwork will be made more durable and easy to maintain if it is painted with, preferably, an oil-based paint or varnished in order to seal its surface.

Bare wooden floors, scrubbed clean or varnished for easy maintenance, can give your bathroom that ultimate country feel. And why not include a colorful rag rug for a better effect and more comfort? The addition of a nonslip back will keep it safely in place even on the highest of gloss finishes. If there are children in the house, then more water may end up on the floor than in the tub. If so, then cork might be a more appropriate and waterproof type of floor covering.

ACCESSORIES AND FURNITURE

A wooden towel rod, the Victorian style of freestanding rail especially, always looks particularly fine in a country-style bathroom, while a wall-mounted mirror is generally considered an essential item. A mirror with a deep wooden frame can look extremely handsome. A large wall mirror, or, better still, more than one, may also create the impression that the room is larger than it in fact is. If you have the luxury of a large bathroom – a conversion from a spare bedroom, perhaps, or a purpose-built extension – you also have the opportunity of introducing other wooden furniture. A small table or a chest of drawers, for example, could be a real asset. The table, with a wood-framed mirror on top, might serve as a dresser, while the drawers will provide welcome storage for towels and toiletries. And if there is room, why not install a comfortable chair?

These items of furniture need not be new, in the best of condition, or even bought specifically for the bathroom. Unwanted pieces from other rooms in the house can be used. A coat of paint will hide a multitude of past scratches, gouges, and rough handling.

Left - HALF-HEIGHT PINE PANELING PARTLY COVERS THE RAGSTONE WALLS OF THIS BATHROOM IN A CONVERTED BARN IN KENT, ENGLAND. THE BATH TUB DATES FROM THE 19TH CENTURY.

Above - THE LEDGED AND BRACED DOOR IS MADE FROM PITCHED PINE RECLAIMED FROM INDUSTRIAL BUILDING DEMOLITION. IT CAME TO BRITAIN FROM THE UNITED STATES AS RETURN CARGO ON SHIPS DELIVERING MANUFACTURED GOODS DURING THE INDUSTRIAL REVOLUTION IN THE 19TH CENTURY.

SHAKER SHELVES &
PEGBOARD

No book dealing with country woodworking techniques would be complete without a detailed look at the work of the American Shaker communities. This utopian religious movement – correctly, but rather long-windedly, known as The United Society of Believers in Christ's Second Appearance – originated in France, but was led in the late 18th century by Ann Lee, the illiterate wife of a blacksmith from Manchester, England, who immigrated to the United States in 1774. Two years later, in 1776, she founded the parent Shaker community at Niskayuna, about seven miles from Albany, New York.

The Shakers, whose name derives from their agitated form of ritual dancing, are best known today for the excellence and simplicity of the work of their craftspeople. One part of the Shaker belief is that work is a form of sacred devotion. Within their strict creed – "hands to work and hearts to God" – they created a simple beauty in all they did; functionalism was predominant, and ornamentation was regarded as unnecessary "worldly show." Their furniture was plain, but always beautifully proportioned; and although it partly reflected influences from the outside world, these were restricted and refined into a style that is uniquely Shaker.

Of their many endeavors, the Shakers are perhaps best known for their fine furniture and wooden artefacts. Many of today's top furniture and interior designers have embraced the purity of Shaker form and style. At first, the Shakers' objective was self-sufficiency, but in due course, what they made became much sought after by the "outside world," and before long they were producing not only what they needed themselves, but also a variety of items for sale.

The simple utility of the hanging set of shelves seen here is typical of Shaker work. Shelves very much like these were made for use in all living and working areas of the house to hold personal effects, kitchen utensils, and objects pertaining to work. As is evident from the photograph, their furniture is entirely functional, yet it combines practicality with a timeless elegance.

The manner in which the shelves are hung is a common Shaker practice. Rooms were routinely fitted with horizontal pegboards. These were often in continuous lengths and set at a uniform height, and so they constitute an important architectural as well as social element in Shaker interiors. Used to accommodate all manner of objects, pegboards, perhaps above all else, epitomize the Shaker preoccupation with order and cleanliness. Pegboards provided not only permanent positions for such things as shelves, clothing, baskets, and so forth, but also essential temporary accommodation for such larger items of furniture as chairs, to make floor cleaning easier and to create additional floor space when it was required in dual-purpose rooms, which, for example, might see the kitchen instantly transformed into a religious meeting room.

Above - FUNCTIONALITY MARRIED TO AN UNCLUTTERED ELEGANCE ARE HALLMARKS OF THE SHAKER FURNITURE TRADITION. PEGBOARDS ARE THE IDEAL SOLUTION TO STORAGE PROBLEMS, WHETHER FOR HANGING SHELVES OR FOR CLEARING FREESTANDING OBJECTS SUCH AS CHAIRS OUT OF THE WAY.

Right - IN TYPICAL SHAKER FASHION, PEGBOARDS ARE USED FOR HANGING AND PUTTING AWAY ALL MANNER OF THINGS. THE ORIGINAL TURNED WOODEN PEGS HAD DISTINCTIVE SHAPES, WHICH VARIED ACCORDING TO THE SHAKER COMMUNITY OR VILLAGE THAT PRODUCED THEM.

SHELVES

ABILITY LEVEL: Novice

SIZE: 25 x 22 x 7 inches

MATERIALS: Pine, Cherry, Beech

CUTTING LIST:
2 sides
22 x 7 x ⅝ inches

3 shelves
25 x 7 x ⅝ inches

PEGBOARD

ABILITY LEVEL: Novice

SIZE:
(**Pegs**) 5 x 1½ x 1½ inches
(**Board**) 48 x 3½ x ¾ inches

MATERIALS:
(**Pegs**) Cherry, Oak, Maple, Beech
(**Board**) Pine

CUTTING LIST:
(**Pegs**) 3 pieces 5 x 1½ x 1½ inches

(**Board**) 1 piece 48 x 3½ x ¾ inches

See template pattern on page 155 for side pieces.

All measurements are given in inches.

SHELVES METHOD:

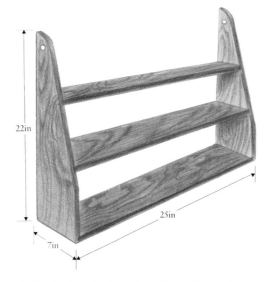

1. Begin by planing the edges of the shelves and gluing pieces together to make wider boards if necessary (see page 141 for advice). Note that the shelves decrease in width toward the top: the middle shelf is approximately 6 inches wide, while the top shelf measures about 5 inches.

2. Cut all pieces accurately to length, making sure that they are perfectly square across their ends.

3. Depending on the condition of the wood, plane or sand back all the surfaces so that they are smooth to the touch.

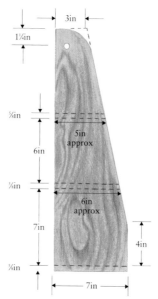

4. Cut both side pieces to the correct tapering shape as shown and plane or sand back the sawn edges.

5. Referring to the diagram, mark out the positions of the top and middle shelf dado and the rabbet to accommodate the bottom shelf. Carefully check the exact thickness of the shelves before doing this, since all dimensions quoted when buying wood may be nominal only. Make the dado fractionally less than the shelf thickness to ensure a tight fit later on.

6. Cut the dadoes and rabbet ¼ inch deep and to the full width of the shelf (see page 142 for advice on cutting dadoes).

7. Check each shelf for correct fit. If it is necessary, remove wood from the underside of the shelves.

8. Drill a ¼-inch hole, as shown, at the top of each side piece for the hanging cords. Before drilling, place a piece of scrap wood under the exit point of the bit to prevent the wood from splintering.

9. Assemble the shelves, without using glue, to make sure that everything fits together properly. Disassemble.

10. Glue and assemble the shelves. If necessary, hold them together with clamps and check that all the angles are square. Wipe off any excess glue.

11. Further secure the bottom rabbet joint by careful nailing. Be very careful not to split the wood (see page 141 for advice on nailing). If the other joints fit tightly and are also nailed together for security, clamping may not be necessary.

12. The shelves illustrated are made of pine and have been painted (see pages 146-7 for different finishing methods).

PEGBOARD METHOD:

1. Pegs would normally be turned on a lathe (dimensions are given in the diagram below). Simple peg shapes can be whittled by hand, however, and finished off by filing and sanding. Alternatively, you can purchase ready-made pegs.

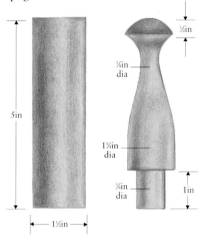

2. If you are turning the pegs on a lathe, place each piece of wood in turn between the centers or anchor each one to a chuck and turn to the shape shown – or any shape of your choice. Make sure that the tenon joint is true to size and is not too small.

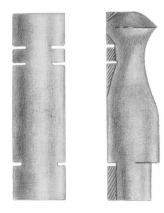

3. If you are shaping the pegs by hand, make preliminary saw cuts all around as shown, and then cut or chisel into these to establish the rough shape of each peg before using files or rasps followed by abrasives to refine the shape.

4. To measure the size of the tenons needed, make a test hole of the correct diameter in a piece of scrap wood.

5. If using ready-made pegs, buy them first and check the diameter of the tenon joints before proceeding to the next stage.

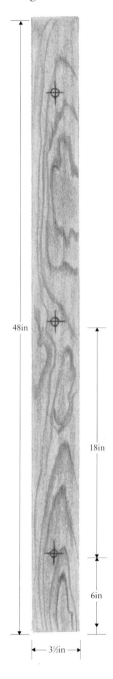

6. Mark the positions of the pegs and drill 1-inch holes (or holes of other sizes to suit) through the board. Drill into a piece of scrap wood to prevent the underside of the board from splintering.

7. Try the pegs for size, without using glue.

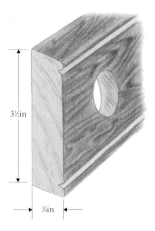

8. Plane or sand the board smooth. It can be left plain or you can bead its edges using a simple beading tool.

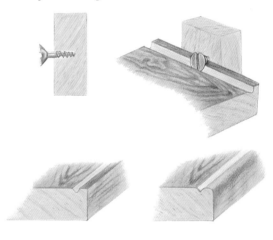

9. As the diagram shows, a beading tool is easy to make out of a screw and a piece of scrap wood. When finished, round off the outer edge with a small plane.

10. Paint the board in your choice of color; keep the paint out of the holes, however, as this will inhibit glue adhesion.

11. Treat the pegs with an oil or other clear finish, avoiding the joint area.

12. When the paint or other finish is dry, glue the pegs into position. When the glue is dry, saw off any protruding tenon joint at the back.

13. You can mount the pegboard by drilling and screwing it to an existing wall. Countersink the screw heads for a neat finish (see page 141 for advice), and then fill and paint over them. On a new wall, pegboards can be partly recessed into the plasterwork.

Cradles were once so commonly used that they transcended social boundaries and were to be found in the poorest as well as the wealthiest of homes. And because of their associations with infancy and childhood, and the custom of their successive use from one generation to the next, many have become cherished objects, even family heirlooms, irrespective of their origins or the quality of their design and construction. Sadly, the very earliest types of cradle have not survived the passage of time. These cradles were not made of wood but were woven – straw, rush, willow, and any other pliable material have all been used successfully for cradle making – in fact, the word for cradle comes from an Old High German word, *kratto,* which means "basket." The Gaelic name, *cliabhan,* literally means "little basket." The biblical basket in which the baby Moses was traditionally hidden and carried downstream was a cradle, and modern wickerwork cradles are sometimes still called Moses baskets.

Some of the earliest known European wooden cradles were simple open boxes. They were made to swing between two uprights to keep the cradles suspended above damp and often unhygienic floors. This type of swing cradle went out of use during the 16th and 17th centuries, but they appear to have made a comeback in Europe during the early 18th century and later became highly fashionable.

In the interim, cradles mounted on rockers and placed on the floor came into common use, and this basic design has remained popular ever since. Some examples had paneled sides, like the chests of the time,

with rockers forming an integral part of the end panel or inserted into the lower end of the corner posts.

The tops of the corner posts often had turned knobs or finials, which proved useful as something to hold onto when rocking the baby to and fro, and, apparently, for winding wool. Some old cradles have small knobs running along the sides, and these were probably used to secure the covers in place. During the 17th century in particular, cradles were usually made of oak, but beech, elm, and various fruitwoods were sometimes used. They were frequently decorated either with carvings of stylized flowers or geometric motifs, and initials and a date were often incorporated. Decorative wood inlay was also popular, and holly and boxwood were often used to good effect for this technique.

Other examples were simpler in concept and had solid-boarded sides and ends, often of pine. The rockers in this case form separate cross bearers and were placed just a few inches in from the ends. In mild climates, where few bedclothes were required, cradles had shallow sides. In colder areas, cradles were made with deeper sides, to cut down on drafts and provide room for more bedding. Many of both designs had hoods. These provided both for extra protection from drafts and also, in the poorer households, from falling debris and drips from unsound roofs. For ease of access, the hood was often hinged so that it could be folded back out of the way. The cradle described here is of the solid, boarded variety and has a simple hinged hood.

Left - AMONG THE INTERESTING COLLECTION OF WOODEN FURNITURE AND WOVEN ARTEFACTS FOUND TOGETHER IN A SWEDISH MOUNTAIN FARMHOUSE IS A CRUDELY MADE, SLAB-SIDED ROCKING CRADLE OF UNUSUAL DESIGN. IT CLEARLY REFLECTS THE TRADITIONS OF A REMOTE REGION.

Above - THIS SOLID-BOARDED VARIETY OF CRADLE HAS A SIMPLE HINGED HOOD. IT IS BASED ON AN IRISH FARMHOUSE CRADLE DATING FROM THE LATE 19TH CENTURY. PAINTED IN A DARK RED-BROWN COLOR, IT CLEARLY SHOWS THE WEAR AND TEAR OF SEVERAL GENERATIONS OF USE.

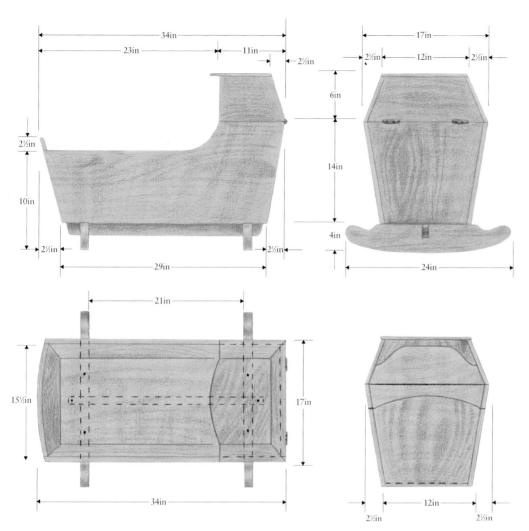

METHOD:

1. Make the body of the cradle first. Use wide boards if possible or edge-join narrow boards to make the required widths (see page 141).

2. Mark and cut out the side pieces as shown and clean up the sawn edges.

3. Mark and cut out the two end pieces and clean up the sawn edges.

4. The sides are joined to the ends using glue and either nails or screws. Screws are preferred. Nails should be 1½-inch finishing nails or oval nails, knocked in dovetail fashion for extra security.

5. To use screws, drill and counterbore the side pieces (see page 141).

6. Screw the sides and ends together without using glue to check that they fit correctly, then disassemble for the next stage.

7. Apply glue to the joint areas and join the sides and ends. Wipe off surplus glue, check that the cradle body is square, and leave to dry. Plug the screw holes and clean off flush or punch nails below the surface and fill.

ABILITY LEVEL: Intermediate

SIZE: 34 x 17 x 20 inches

MATERIALS: Pine, Cherry, Oak

CUTTING LIST:

2 sides
34 x 14 x ¾ inches

1 top end
17 x 14 x ¾ inches

1 lower end
15½ x 12½ x ¾ inches

1 bottom
27½ x 12½ x ½ inches

2 hood sides
11 x 6 x ¾ inches

See template patterns on page 153 for cradle rocker and hood arch.

All measurements are given in inches.

1 hood back
17 x 6 x ¾ inches

1 hood arch
17 x 4 x ¾ inches

1 hood top
14 x 10 x ½ inches

2 rockers
24 x 4 x 1 inches

1 brace
27 x 2 x ¾ inches

8. Prepare the cradle bottom. Cut this oversize to the inside measurements across the bottom of the cradle initially. Then, fitting from the top, trim it to a bevel edge all around to obtain a wedge fit, flush with the bottom edges of the cradle body.

9. When this is achieved, glue and anchor the bottom in position with brads, and leave it until the glue is dry.

10. When the glue is dry, trim the joined edges of the cradle body flush and round over any sharp corners.

11. Plane the top edges of the cradle body even with where the hood will fit.

12. Now make the hood. The dimensions in the cutting list are only a guide; use the actual measurements taken from your cradle, since they may differ slightly.

13. Mark and cut out the back piece first to establish the shape of the hood. From these same outside dimensions, mark out and cut the arch piece.

14. Cut the inside shape of the arch piece and round over its inside edge (see template pattern on page 153).

15. Mark and cut out the two side pieces.

16. Bevel the top and bottom edges of the back and side hood components to improve the contact with the cradle body and with the flat top, when it is attached. Do this with a plane and don't worry if mating bevels are not perfect.

17. Holding them temporarily together, check that the hood back and sides fit and match up correctly on the cradle body. Adjust if necessary; take care not to make the hood components too small.

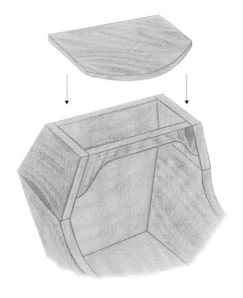

18. Glue and nail (or screw) the hood components together. Check that the shape of the hood still fits the cradle body and that it is square. Wipe off surplus glue and leave it to dry. Plug the screw holes and clean off flush or conceal nails.

19. Cut to size and attach the flat top. Glue and brads are sufficient, but avoid splitting the wood (see page 141).

20. Clean up the completed hood by planing joined edges flush and rounding over any sharp corners.

21. The hood is hinged to the cradle body (see page 102, step 20 for advice on hinges).

22. Now make and fit the rockers. Cut out the two rockers (see template on page 153) and clean up the sawn edges. Round over the rocking edges so that they don't become "carpet cutters." Cut out for the half lap joint with the center brace (see page 143).

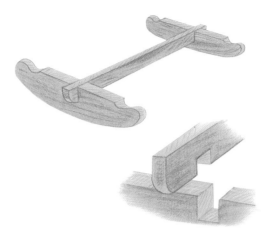

23. Cut the center brace to size and shape and clean up the sawn edges. Cut out for the half lap joints with rockers.

24. Try the half lap joints for fit and adjust them if necessary.

25. Stand the cradle on the rockers/brace assembly and measure and mark its position on the inside of the cradle bottom.

26. Drill and countersink two holes along the line of each rocker and three holes along the line of the brace, as shown.

27. Fit the rockers and brace in position with screws through the bottom of the cradle.

28. Round over any remaining sharp edges and sand everything to a smooth finish. Apply a suitable stain, varnish or paint inside and out as required (see page 146-7 for advice on finishing methods).

The family chest, to which this chest is a kind of country cousin, is regarded by many as being the earliest form of furniture. Like its forerunners, it is primarily designed for storage, but such boxes once fulfilled an essential multipurpose role in the homes of our ancestors. In addition to holding clothing and bed linen and such valuables as documents and silver plate, they also served as seat, table and, sometimes, even as bed in what were very sparsely furnished homes of the time. Furthermore, the chest was always packed and ready to travel, and it could even be very quickly hidden away and kept safe in times of social and political unrest and upheaval.

The most primitive chests were of the "dug-out" variety, and were little more than hollowed-out tree trunks – hence the use, still common today, of the name "trunk" to mean a large piece of luggage or a traveling box. Thankfully, the modern descendants weigh far less than their predecessors did. As woodworking techniques improved and became more sophisticated, rough-hewn oak boards were joined at the corners with hand-wrought nails, and the case itself was heavily banded with iron straps – as much to stop the structure from falling apart as for the security of its contents. Few chests of this type remain today; often they stood on damp stone floors, which eventually caused the wood to rot. The ironwork fared little better, since the combination of damp and the tannic acid from the oak corroded the metal.

During the 14th century, vertical end pieces known as stiles were added. These had grooves that held the ends of the now-thinner, horizontal boards, making a stronger structure. When they were extended below the chest, these stiles became legs that raised the chest off the floor. During this period and later, chests became lighter in construction, with side planks an inch or less in thickness. Some chests were also made without stiles and instead had their ends joined by dovetailing.

The big leap forward in the chest development came in the early 15th century with the introduction of frame and panel construction. Using this technique, mortised and tenoned frames have grooves in them so that panels are held in position without nails or glue and are free to expand and contract without harming the structure as a whole. In due time, of course, the chest was to develop into the chest of drawers – but that is another story.

The boarded chest or box remained in use, however, particularly in rural areas. In time it, too, was improved by being made of seasoned wood. Chests became generally lighter in construction and had their ends joined not by nailing but by a return to dovetail jointing.

The multipurpose role of chests also continued, for boxes of this type were used in all manner of ways – as tool boxes and boxes for books and blankets, as well as for the storage of personal belongings, animal feed, and illicit alcohol. Their continued popularity was due in part to the fact that they were inexpensive to make, compared with a lavish, complicated and more costly chest of drawers, and partly to the fact that, in places where prepared wood was scarce and woodworking experience in short supply, chests and boxes were economical in terms of both materials and skill.

Above - A SIMPLY AND SOLIDLY MADE BLANKET CHEST CONSTRUCTED FROM WIDE BOARDS OF PINE. STANDING AT THE FOOT OF A RUSTIC-STYLE BED, IT CONTINUES A LONG TRADITION OF PROVIDING USEFUL STORAGE SPACE FOR BEDDING. THE SIDES ARE STRONGLY JOINED TOGETHER BY INTERLOCKING DOVETAILS.

Right - BOXES OF ALL KINDS WERE IN FAR GREATER USE IN EARLIER TIMES, AND THIS COLLECTION SHOWS SOMETHING OF THE DIVERSITY OF THEIR DESIGN. MOST ARE PINE WITH A PAINTED FINISH; SOME, PERHAPS ORIGINALLY LEATHER-BOUND, ARE STUDDED WITH DECORATIVE BRASS NAILS.

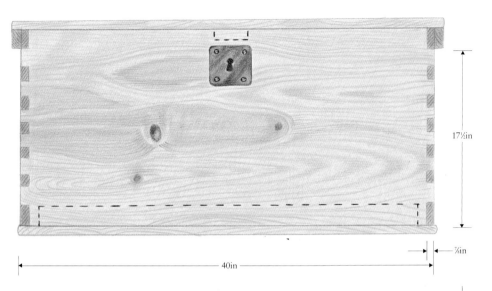

17½in

40in

⅞in

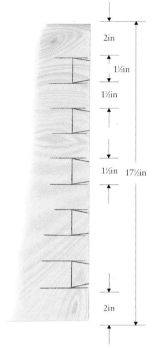

2in

1½in

1½in

1½in

1½in

17½in

2in

ABILITY LEVEL: Intermediate/
Experienced

SIZE: 40 x 18 x 19 inches

MATERIALS: Pine, Cedar

CUTTING LIST:
2 sides
40 x 17½ x ⅞ inches

2 ends
18 x 17½ x ⅞ inches

1 top
42 x 18 x ⅞ inches

1 bottom
40 x 18 x ⅞ inches

4 end battens
18 x 2 x ⅞ inches

3 long battens
40 x 2 x ⅞ inches

1 center batten
17 x 3 x ⅞ inches

Pair "T" hinges

Brass box lock with brass plate
4 x 4 inches

All measurements are given in inches.

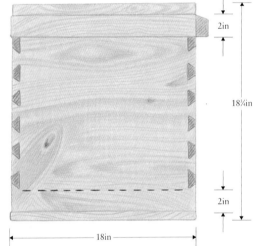

2in

18¾in

2in

18in

METHOD:

1. Ideally, this project should be made, as the original was, from single wide boards. If you can't locate suitable boards, you will have to edge-join narrower ones to make up the required widths (see page 141 for advice).

2. Cut the two long sides and two end pieces to the correct width and length and make sure the ends are square. Select the face sides and keep these facing outward. Leave the top and bottom pieces a little oversize at this stage; these will be trimmed to fit after the side and end pieces are assembled to make the main carcass.

3. Carefully mark out the "tails" of the dovetail joints on the end pieces (see page 143) using the measurements given. Note: top and bottom tails are the largest at 2 inches;

all the others are equal divisions of 1½ inches. Cut out the "tails."

4. Using the "tails" as a template, mark out and cut the "pins" or sockets (see page 143).

5. Test fit the mating dovetails, but not too often, and adjust as necessary.

6. Prepare for assembly by cleaning surface marks and guidelines from the sides and ends, inside and out. Have clamps ready at hand, but if the joints are tight-fitting, these may not be necessary.

7. Glue the sides and ends to make the main carcass. Clamp up, if required, and check that the work is square. Wipe off surplus glue and leave it to dry.

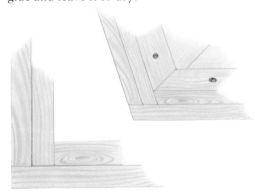

8. Cut to the correct size two of the end battens and two of the long battens and fix them to the inside of the carcass, flush with the bottom edge. Glue and screw, or nail, the battens into place.

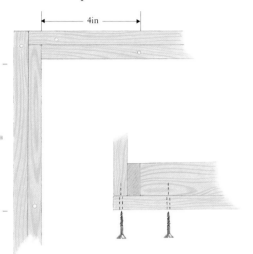

9. Trim the bottom to fit the outside dimensions of the carcass. Secure it in place with countersunk screws, staggering them as shown at about 4-inch intervals on the ends, and at 8-inch intervals along the sides.

10. This method of attaching the bottom is true to the original rather than being the best technique. A better method is to trim the bottom to fit inside the carcass so that it rests on the battens fitted on the inside.

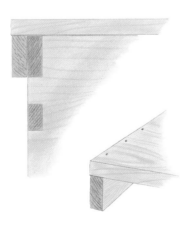

11. Now cut the top to size. It should match the outside dimensions across the width of the carcass but overhang the two end battens (when fitted) so that it does not interfere with the ends of the carcass when the lid is closed (see detail).

12. Cut the two end battens to size and attach them to the top as shown, by gluing and screwing, or nailing. Clean up the sawn edges and smooth over the sharp corners.

13. Cut the center batten (3 inches) to fit, without interference, the inside dimension across the width of the carcass. Fit this square across the inside surface of the top. Use glue and screws for the strength needed when the lock is fitted.

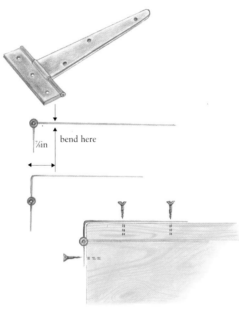

bend here

14. The original chest had long, cranked hinges to secure the top to the carcass. These are now difficult to obtain, but you can use modern "T" hinges instead. Modify these by carefully bending them as shown, or use ordinary butt hinges instead (see page 102, step 20 for advice on fitting hinges).

15. Make sure that the top closes without straining the hinges. Some adjustment may be required.

16. Attach the remaining long batten to the back of the box – flush with the top edge – using glue and screws, or nails. Lightly chamfer the top edge of the batten away from the carcass before attaching it and cut away some of the wood at the hinge positions. This batten prevents the top from swinging back too far when opened.

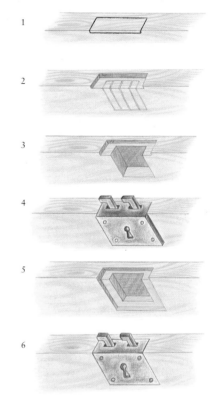

17. Follow the numbered illustrations for attaching a heavy-duty lock to the chest. Locate its position and drill through for the key hole. Then, on the inside, chisel out a recess to accommodate the body of the lock. The catch plate, which is supplied with the lock, is attached to the underside of the top, close to the center batten.

18. After attaching the lock, a brass plate measuring 4 x 4 inches with a suitable key hole can be screwed to the outside, to imitate the original lock plate.

19. When everything is complete, clean off all surface marks and smooth any rough edges, and then apply the finish of your choice. The original had a stained finish, details of which are on page 146. If you have used cedar, leave the inside untreated since the odor of the wood deters moths.

FOLK BED

W hile Egyptian pharaohs slept on elaborate feline-footed beds of inlaid ebony and ivory, and Roman emperors reclined on couches covered in silk, the beds of our more immediate ancestors were little more than rough pallets or straw-filled mattresses. During the so-called Dark Ages in Europe, when one large room served for both living and sleeping, these beds were simply spread on the floor or laid on chests or benches. Some would have been placed in recesses built into the wall, a little like ships' berths. However, even after separate but shared sleeping chambers were introduced, for lesser members of the household, the mattress was the only bed they had.

Wealthier families placed their mattresses on wooden boards raised off the ground, away from drafts and vermin, on bedsteads. Our modern word *bed* is, in fact, a contraction of *bedstead*, meaning "the place of the bed." These bedstocks, as they were known, consisted of a framework of four rails joined to short corner posts that formed the legs. Later, these rails were drilled with holes through which cords or webbing could be threaded to support the mattress.

From this period onward, beds developed in various ways, the best known being those that included the use of draperies around the bed, which later led to what we now call the four-poster. These draperies served a practical purpose; as well as just looking decorative, they provided both warmth and privacy for the rich and noble. Initially, bed curtains were hung directly from the ceiling or from a suspended framework known as a tester. Later the tester was supported on four corner posts, which, in due course, became incorporated into the bed frame itself. However, it was the development from the simple bedstock, of what became known in the 18th century as the stump bedstead – in which the turned or square legs of the wooden framework were extended at one end and filled in with a plain headboard – that provided the basic design for so many other beds. The supporting wooden laths, which had replaced the corded or webbed base, had by this time given way to the use of spring metal, and by the middle of the 19th century, the iron and brass bedstead had become fashionable. Country makers, however, continued to make wooden bedsteads, and today they remain as popular as ever.

Left - THIS SOLIDLY MADE, SUBSTANTIAL BED, WITH BOTH CURVED HEAD- AND FOOTBOARDS, HAS A DISTINCTLY FOLK-ART FEEL TO IT. IT IS MADE FROM NATURAL FINISHED PINE. THE TWO HEART-SHAPED CUTOUTS ARE A TYPICAL DECORATIVE MOTIF OF THE TIROL REGION IN THE SWISS ALPS.

ABILITY LEVEL: Experienced

SIZE: 80 x 56 x 44 inches

MATERIALS: Pine

CUTTING LIST:
2 corner posts
44 x 3 x 3 inches

2 corner posts
34 x 3 x 3 inches

1 head board
53 x 32 x ¼ inches

1 foot board
53 x 22 x ¼ inches

2 side rails
77 x 6 x 1½ inches

2 slat rails
75 x 2 x 1 inches

12 slats
52 x 3 x 1 inches

4 wooden balls
3 inches

4 bolts
6 inches

These dimension are designed for a 75 x 54-inch mattress. It is best to measure the mattress to be used, however, before starting this project and adjust dimensions as necessary.

See template pattern on page 153 for heart motif.

All measurements are given in inches.

NOTE After cleaning off all surface marks, you can apply a clear polish, stain or paint (see pages 146-7 for different finishes).

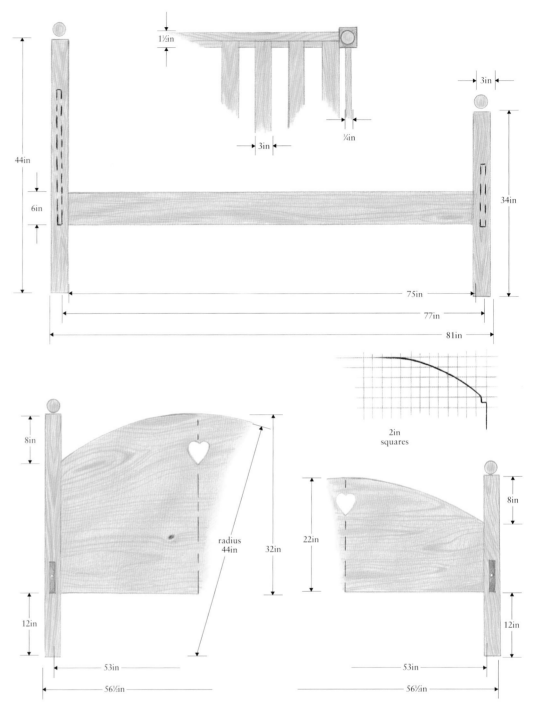

METHOD:

1. Begin by making the head and foot boards by edge-joining narrower pieces of wood (see page 141 for advice). Individual pieces should be as wide as possible so that there are not too many joints.

2. When gluing is complete and the work has dried, clean up the boards and check that they are flat. Cut them to the exact length and check that the ends are square.

3. Mark and cut out the curved top edge of each board. Round over the cut edges.

4. Mark and cut out the heart motifs. Use the template on page 153.

5. Cut the corner posts to length and plane or sand the surfaces smooth. The ball finials are optional and may be fitted later. Make pencil marks on one end of the posts, as shown at the top of page 133, to avoid confusion later when marking out for jointing.

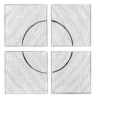

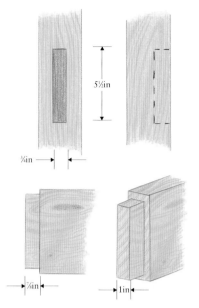

6. Head and foot boards are housed, at their full thickness, in mortises cut into the corner posts. Take measurements from the boards you have; these may differ from those given. Make the mortises a little undersized and trim the ends of the boards to a tight fit.

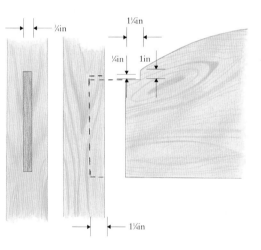

7. Each end board is notched at the top to fit the mortise and should be cut slightly short (see diagram). This is an allowance for any movement that may take place in the boards.

8. Test fit the end boards individually, without using glue, in their respective slots. Adjust if necessary by trimming the ends of the boards until the joints are tight and enter to their full depth. Disassemble and put the boards aside until later.

9. Mark the correct adjacent face of each corner post for the mortises to accommodate the side rails. The pencil marks made on the end of the posts will help here. Cut out these mortises (see page 144 for advice).

10. Cut the side rails to length and make sure that the ends are square. Plane or sand the rails smooth.

11. Mark and cut out the tenons on each end of the side rails (see page 144 for advice).

12. Test fit the side rail tenons and the corner post mortises, without using glue. Adjust as necessary for a good fit.

13. The head and foot boards are permanently glued into their corner post joints. The side rail tenons are not glued but held in their corner post mortises by bed bolts, as shown, to allow easy assembly and a useful knock-down facility. Bolts can be bought or made using threaded studding.

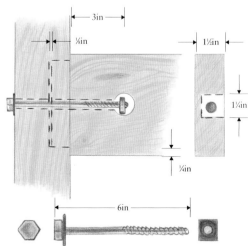

14. The diagrams show how to fit the bed bolts, but measurements may need to be altered to suit the bolts actually used. The nut recess is bored on the inside of the side rail. Place the post on its side on a bench,

with the rail tenon in place in its mortise, and bore the through hole carefully with a carpenter's twist bit.

15. Try each joint by fitting the bolt and nut and tightening it until the shoulders of the rail tenon come up tight against the corner post. Make identification marks on the rails and posts to aid reassembly. Disassemble for the next stage.

16. To attach the ball finials, if required, find the center of the corner posts and bore a hole to house the fixing dowel. Glue in place.

17. Chamfer the long edges of each corner post and, if finials are not fitted, round over the top edges.

18. Now join the end boards to their respective corner posts. Place glue in the slot mortises, fit the end boards correctly, and pull them in tight with clamps. Clean off any surplus glue. Leave to dry.

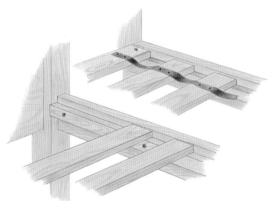

19. The mattress rests on slats, which are supported on rails glued and screwed to the inside of the side rails. Attach these rails so that the slats will be flush with, or slightly below, the top edge of the side rails.

20. Now assemble the bed frame. Make sure that the side rails fit into their correct mortises and that the bed bolts are tightened up fully. Cut the slats to fit across the frame. Space them out evenly. Slats may be loosely strung together, nailed, or stapled to two lengths of woven tape. Screw the top and bottom slats down and the whole assembly will stay in place.

Tools & Techniques

Most of the projects featured in this book require only the simplest of woodworking tools, so there is no need to have or buy expensive or complicated equipment. Some basic knowledge of how to use these tools is assumed, however. If you are a beginner at woodworking, start with the projects designed for the "novice" level; by working through these, hopefully you will soon pick up the expertise required to undertake the more complicated "intermediate" and "experienced" projects.

All of the projects have been designed to be completed using hand tools only. Although immensely satisfying, working entirely with hand tools (as opposed to power tools) can be both tiring and time-consuming, as well as often requiring a high degree of skill. If, however, you have power tools available – and you know how to use them safely and competently – there is no reason why you should not press them into service. In my own work I often use a combination of methods: power tools for the initial, often repetitive, work such as sawing to size and planing to thickness; a combination of power and hand tools for shaping and jointing; and hand tools for finishing and detailing.

The original country woodworker would have had few tools at his disposal, and these would have most probably been general-purpose implements, rather than specialist ones, used for all manner of jobs around the cottage or farm. An ax and an adze would have been used for chopping and riving, for example; a saw and a few chisels for cutting; a drawknife, spokeshave, rasp, and files for shaping; a plane for smoothing; a brace and bit for drilling holes; a hammer and nails for fastening; and a knife for cutting and trimming.

Construction methods, too, would have been all-purpose and relatively simple, using whatever wood was available and most suitable for the job in hand. The fundamental techniques of woodworking – shaping and jointing – have been known for thousands of years, and working methods evolved from applications such as house and barn construction, fence building, wheelmaking, and so on. The joints used were basic to all forms of woodworking: the mortise and tenon of the shipwright and barn framer is larger and perhaps cruder than that of the furniture maker, but it is the same joint; the foot-long trenels (tree nails) of the trestle builder are no different in principle to the smaller pegs used to secure the joints of a country-made chair.

The techniques employed in the projects section of this book would have been used as a matter of course by the early country woodworker, and while the methods of certain types of construction may not have been part of the daily routine, he would certainly have been familiar with them. However, the exact way and sequence in which the steps are carried out would no doubt have varied according to an individual's knowledge and level of skill. In the projects described, the methods given follow traditional principles that are accepted and in use today, but they are open to individual interpretation.

BASIC TOOLS

It is not easy to say what a basic set of tools is for a modern woodworker — much depends on what is to be made, on personal preferences, and what is affordable. But whatever you decide on, always buy the best quality you can afford, and then take good care of the tools that you have. Working with poorly made or misused tools is a handicap nobody needs.

The list that follows includes those tools required for the projects and it concentrates mainly on hand tools, together with a few of the most helpful and time-saving power tools. You can add more tools as and when the need for them arises.

BASIC HAND TOOLS

Tape measure
Rule
Marking knife
Carpenter's or combination square
Sliding T-bevel
Pencils
Marking gauge

Crosscut or combination saw
Coping saw and blades for coping saw
Small back saw

Smoothing plane No. 4
Spokeshave
Wood chisels
Block plane
Cabinet scraper
Curved carving gouge

Mallet
Pincers
Screwdrivers
Cross peen hammer, or claw hammer
Nail set

Drill
Twist drills/Forstner bits
Awl

Rasp, half round
File, half round

Clamps

Sharpening stones

OPTIONAL POWER TOOLS

Electric drill
Orbital sander
Jigsaw or band saw
Power router

DRAWINGS AND PATTERNS

Before undertaking any project in wood, it is helpful to have a drawing or plan showing the general shape and main dimensions of the piece, preferably including more detailed drawings of specific parts. There are two main ways in which such drawings as these may be presented.

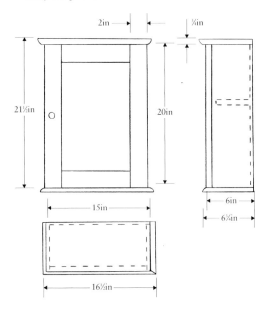

The first is known as an orthographic presentation, which normally shows three views – front and end views, plus a top, or plan, view.

The second form of presentation is a perspective drawing, which may also be in the form of an "exploded" view.

Sometimes it is helpful to show detailed parts of a project, such as curves, as a pattern or template. Where these cannot be shown full size, they are drawn on a scale grid. Each small square of the grid represents 1 inch or 2 inches, as indicated, and from this you can lay out a full-sized pattern using grid squares of the correct size.

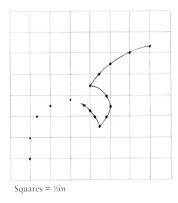

Squares = ⅛in

WORKBENCH AND VISE

On the practical side, a space in which to work and a sturdy table or bench are your first requirements. This bench or table should also have some reliable method of holding wood securely while you are working on it. This usually means fitting a vise of some type, but you can also use other devices, such as bench stops or dogs and C clamps of various sizes.

A cast-iron carpenter's vise with wooden jaw facings is ideal. If, however, you have an engineer's vise, you will need to cover its iron jaws to prevent them from biting into and damaging the wood. For light work, you can temporarily clamp a vise to the edge of your bench.

Another useful device is a bench-hook, which you can easily make yourself. It can be gripped in a vise or held against the edge of your bench to provide a useful holding stop for work being chiseled or sawn, as well as helping to prevent damage to the bench top during these operations.

MEASURING AND MARKING OUT

Before you start making up any piece, you need to check that the wood is the right size and that it is straight and square and not warped. If you buy wood "surfaced," it should be fine to work with, but its machine-planed surface will require further hand planing or sanding. Identify the best wide surface and an edge, plane them square if necessary, and then mark them with face-side and face-edge marks. From then on, all marking out and gauging should be done on or from these surfaces.

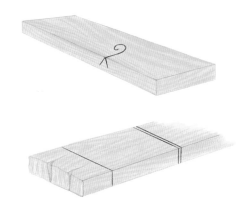

When you need to cut a board to length, make certain to check that the starting end is sound (not damaged or split) as well as square. If necessary, mark off a "waste" piece from the suspect end, measuring the length of the board from that mark. For a small board you can use a rule, but a retractable steel tape is quicker when measuring a long board.

When drawing the line to indicate the length of board you want, mark it accurately and squarely by using a carpenter's square or an all-metal combination square. For precise work, make an allowance for the width of the saw cut, or kerf. Always saw on the waste side of the line, and if you want to cut several pieces from the same board, allow a generous ⅛ inch waste strip for the kerf between each piece.

A well-sharpened No. 2 pencil is suitable for most of the marking out you will encounter. But, for really accurate results, the point of a sharp knife has many advantages, especially when marking wood across the grain. The knife point severs the surface fibers of the wood and leaves a clean edge after cutting. A traditional carpenter's marking knife has a thick, beveled skew blade for this purpose – usually ground for right-hand users only. A small, lock-blade pocket knife is also recommended.

To mark lines parallel to an edge, you should use a marking gauge, which is mainly used to gauge wood to both width and thickness prior to hand planing. Adjust it to give the mark you need by setting the required distance between the movable head and the pointed spur. To mark a line, press the head firmly against the edge of the work and push or pull the gauge away from you. Use a light stroke to reduce the danger of the point digging in and following the grain.

For less precise work, hold a pencil and your fingers as shown – this "trick of the trade" is known as finger gauging.

There are two other types of gauge you should be familiar with: the cutting gauge and the mortise gauge. The cutting gauge has a small blade instead of the marking gauge's spur, and it is most effective when marking across the grain. The mortise gauge, as its name suggests, is mainly used for marking out mortise and tenon joints. It has two pointed spurs – the inner one is adjustable so that you can mark out parallel lines of different distances from each other.

Compasses and dividers are most often used to mark circles or arcs, and you can use dividers to transfer measurements and to "step-off" equal divisions along a line.

SAWS AND SAWING

There are several different types of hand saw, some designed for general use and others for more specialized applications. The shape and size of the saw blade, and the number and configuration of its teeth, are what distinguish one type from another.

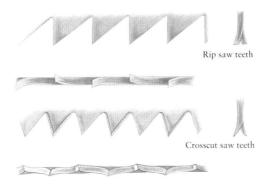

Rip saw teeth

Crosscut saw teeth

Rip saws, for example, are large, have between four and six teeth every 1 inch, and are used for cutting (ripping) with the grain. The shorter crosscut saw has between 7 and 12 teeth every 1 inch. Both types are used mainly in the initial preparation of wood and for cutting boards to size.

The tenon saw is the best-known example of what are called back saws. These saws have thin blades stiffened and weighted by a folded metal strip, usually brass, along their back edges, and they are used for accurate bench work and for cutting joints. Back saws are available in different sizes and can have from 12 to more than 20 teeth every 1 inch. The smallest type of back saw with the greatest number of teeth and finest cut is

generally known as a dovetail saw. Saws for cutting curved shapes use a narrow, flexible blade that breaks easily. In some saws, this problem is overcome by holding the blade under tension in a frame. The earliest type, known as a bow saw, has a blade held in a wooden frame tensioned by means of a twisted cord. More modern designs rely on a spring-steel frame and one of these, the coping saw, uses disposable blades that fit into pins tensioned by twisting the handle of the saw. You can fit the blade so that it cuts either on the pull stroke or on the push stroke. To make an internal cut through a piece of wood, first drill a small hole through the work, pass the blade through, and then fit it into the saw frame. The coping saw is used to remove waste wood from dovetail joints (see page 143).

If you always make sure your saw is sharp, then sawing by hand should not be too difficult. Never force the saw into the wood. This is hard work and tends to cause the blade to twist and jam in the kerf. For trouble-free sawing, support or hold your work securely; work with firm, even, fluid strokes; and use the whole length of the blade to cut with. Begin carefully – with a tenon saw, pull back on the first strokes to establish a start – and work to the waste side of the line.

All of these sawing operations can be carried out with power tools, either portable or fixed. You can use a circular saw for straight cuts, while for straight and curved cuts you have a choice of the versatile jigsaw, saber saw, a machine scroll saw, or a band saw.

PLANES AND PLANING

The type of plane generally known as a bench plane is used to reduce the thickness or width of a piece of wood to the size required and to straighten or smooth a surface. Other types of specialist plane are used for grooving, molding, and shaping; some of these may be multipurpose planes.

There are various types and sizes of bench plane, but they are all constructed in much the same way. Early planes had wooden bodies, or stocks, fitted with a blade, or cutting iron, held in place with a wooden wedge. The all-metal plane appeared in the middle of the 19th century and, due to the fact that it could be more easily and precisely adjusted, it became the preferred tool – although wooden planes are still in use today.

The metal jack plane is a "jack-of-all-trades." Its main use is to bring wood down to size, but if it is fitted with a suitably ground and sharpened blade (see page 140), you can also use it for general straightening and smoothing. The length of a jack plane varies between 14 inches and 18 inches, making it particularly useful for planing long edges for jointing purposes. The metal smoothing plane is made in the same way as the jack plane, but it is shorter in length – 8 inches to 10 inches. It, too, can be used as a general-purpose plane, but it is intended mainly for finishing a surface after a jack plane or a machine plane has been used. Light planing with a sharp and fine-set smoothing plane can produce an excellent surface finish.

When planing a piece of work, make sure that the wood is securely and safely held in place. When edge planing, grip the work in a bench vise; for surface planing, either clamp the wood to the bench top or hold it between pairs of bench dogs. In order to achieve a smooth finish, you have to plane with the grain of the wood, not against it. On the end grain, plane in halfway from each side to avoid splitting out the far edge. The lower cutting angle of the smaller block plane is best for end grain work.

As a general rule, when any plane is not in use, place it on its side on the bench in order to prevent damage to the blade.

For a particularly fine finish, especially on hardwoods, a cabinet scraper is the ideal tool. This device consists simply of a thin piece of good-quality steel, the edge of which is especially shaped and sharpened to

remove a delicate shaving of wood – like a butterfly's wing – when held and flexed between the fingers and thumbs of both hands and pushed forward over the wood at a suitable angle.

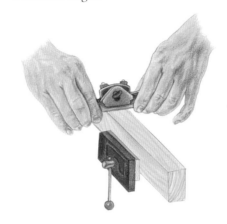

Although a spokeshave is not really a plane, it cuts in a similar way. Older, wooden-stocked spokeshaves have forged, tanged blades, which may be more difficult to adjust than a modern spokeshave but produce an excellent finish. Modern metal spokeshaves are available in either flat or half-round versions. Used with a pushing action, a spokeshave makes chamfers and smooths narrow curved edges. A drawknife, which is used mainly for roughing-out work and for rounding and shaping, is drawn toward you with a firm pulling action. Drawknives are best suited to working on green (unseasoned) wood.

The specialist planes used for such tasks as grooving have become more or less obsolete due to the portable electric router, which does the same work with greater speed. Many of these hand planes are still available, however, and may be used.

Electric planers can be either portable or fixed. Hand-held electric planers are not recommended and stationary machines can be expensive. Wherever possible, it is best to buy wood that is "surfaced" or "prepared" to size. If wood is machine-planed, it will need to be sanded or finished off with a hand plane in order to remove the rippled surface left by the rotary cutting action produced by all power planers.

CHISELS AND GOUGES
Chisels for woodworking are of several different types and come in many different

sizes, depending on the work they are to perform: firmer, bevel-edged, paring, and mortise are just some of the names given to them. "Chisels" with a curved cutting edge should more correctly be called gouges. In addition, there are chisels and gouges made specifically for lathe work and for wood carving. Chisels are categorized by size – for example, the width of the cutting edge – and gouges by size and "sweep" – the degree of curvature of the cutting edge.

For general woodworking, the bevel-edged chisel has some clear advantages over the others, since its shape makes it particularly suitable for reaching into tight corners, cleaning out joints, and so on. You can, if necessary, strike the top of its handle lightly with a wooden mallet to get extra force behind its cutting action. Keep your chisels sharp at all times – it is easier to have an accident when forcing a blunt chisel to cut than when guiding a sharp chisel into the wood. And never hold your piece of work with one hand while using a chisel with the other – secure the wood in place and keep both hands behind the chisel's cutting edge. Make your first cuts across the grain of the wood to sever the fibers and try to cut with the grain at all other times.

SHAPING AND SMOOTHING
Although a cutting tool produces a better surface finish and is satisfying to use, there are times when you need to use other implements for shaping and smoothing. Rasps and files are abrading tools made from hardened steel. Rasps have coarse, triangular-shaped teeth and, because they remove wood quite quickly, they are used for rough shaping.

Files, which come in a variety of "cuts" from coarse to fine, are used more for smoothing. All cuts of files can be bought in flat and half-round shapes – some files in round, or "rat's tail," section.

Modern abrading tools usually have tungsten-carbide grit welded to both rigid and flexible substrates, while another design incorporates a disposable blade of thin, hardened steel perforated with many sharp-edged holes. These holes form multiple cutting edges but they leave a rough surface that requires smoothing.

For many shaping operations, you can use electric belt, disk, and drum sanders, while orbital sanders are often recommended for surface finishing. These devices can save you a lot of time, especially in production work, but they do not always leave a satisfactory finish. They also produce a lot of fine dust. Either the tool should have its own dust bag or you will need to wear a dust-protection mask or respirator.

DRILLS AND DRILLING

Traditionally, wood-boring bits or auger bits fixed into a brace of wood and metal were used for drilling holes in wood. These were replaced by all-metal braces using interchangeable bits, or drills, together with another form of hand drill sometimes called a wheelbrace. Metal braces, some with a ratchet action, and wheelbraces are still in use today, but the portable electric hand drill is now the most popular and commonly used device for drilling holes in wood. You can buy a vertical stand to convert an ordinary electric hand drill into a simple but effective bench drill, while the multispeed drilling machine, available in both bench

and floor-standing models, is more suited to heavy and repetitive work.

Whatever type of drill you decide to use, there is a wide variety of drill bits from which to choose. For general drilling, up to about ½ inch in diameter, ordinary twist bits, or engineer's drills, are suitable (A). An improvement on this design is the modified twist bit known as the dowel bit, or brad point bit (B). For more accurate drilling and for large-diameter holes, the saw-tooth Forstner bit is recommended (C), but this type of drill bit requires a power drill. If you are using a brace, the old type of center bits (D) and auger bits (E) are probably best. For countersinking after drilling, use a rose-head countersink (F).

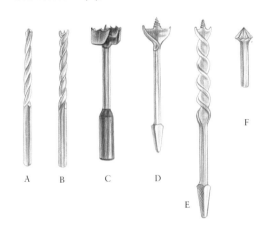

HAMMERS, SCREWDRIVERS, ETC.

For the projects described in this book, a medium-weight cross peen hammer is most generally suitable. Hold small nails and brads between your fingers and start off using the tapered peen before switching to the face of the hammer to drive them home. A claw hammer is also suitable; use a light-weight one for small nails. A pair of pliers is useful for removing nails that bend or break. A wooden mallet is used mainly when you are working with a chisel or gouge, but you may also find it useful at the assembly stage of some jobs. Choose a medium-sized mallet with a head made from seasoned beech.

Screwdrivers are available in a wide choice of sizes and types, with handles in different shapes and made from a variety of materials. What matters most is the size and shape of the end, or tip, in relation to the size and type of screw you are using. The oldest and perhaps the most common type of

screwdriver is the flat-tip blade made to fit the traditional slotted screw heads; more modern types include various patterns of Phillips-head screws and screwdrivers. A flat-tip blade should fit snugly into the screw slot. Make sure that it is neither too large nor too small or you may damage the screw.

For starting screws, and sometimes nails, in softwood you may find an awl useful. An awl makes a guide hole and reduces the danger of the wood splitting. Start a screwdriver-tipped awl across the grain of the wood. When nailing or screwing into hardwood, and sometimes into softwood, it is best to drill clearance and pilot holes (see page 141). You can use a pin punch or nail set to sink nail heads below the surface of your work.

CLAMPS

Clamps are useful items for holding work in place temporarily or for applying pressure to pieces of wood that have been glued while it dries and bonds them together. The most common clamp is the C clamp, and there are several types and sizes from which to choose. The size is usually quoted as the maximum distance between the jaws and

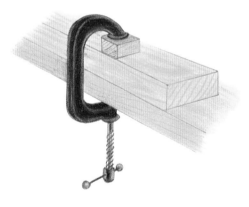

may range from 2 inches to 12 inches. For holding larger or wider pieces of work, usually during the assembly stages, you should use bar clamps. These consist of a steel bar drilled through at intervals to hold a nail that retains a sliding jaw or shoe. At the opposite end of the bar clamp, there is an adjustable jaw that takes up the final pressure. Always use clamps with protective blocks to prevent the surface of your work from being damaged. There are numerous modern variations of both these standard types, some better than others.

ABRASIVES AND ADHESIVES

The words "sandpaper" and "sanding" are still frequently used as general terms for abrasive sheet materials and their use. Sand, however, is no longer to be found on abrasive sheets. Instead, materials such as powdered glass, crushed garnet, aluminum oxide, or silica carbide are used. These are deposited as grits onto various backings – cloth or paper – and in different densities and grit sizes. Sheets are normally classified by the type and grade of abrasive and by a number system related to grit size – the higher the number, the finer the abrasive. For hand sanding, many people prefer pink-colored garnet paper in grades 100, 150, and 220. Always sand with, not across, the grain of the wood, and wrap the paper around a sanding block to help keep the surface of the wood flat. Even if you use a power sander, you will still probably have to finish off by hand sanding.

The term "gluing-up" may in fact mean using any one of numerous adhesives that are now available. Traditionally, animal glue was used – it was all there was – and this had to be melted and applied hot. Today, there are upward of a dozen different types of adhesive, some intended for specialist applications. Those based on PVA (poly-vinyl acetate) are good, general-purpose glues, available in formulations for both indoor and outdoor use. Where a high level of water resistance is required, use a synthetic resin adhesive.

SHARPENING TOOLS

Sharp tools are a prerequisite for producing good-quality work – a dull cutting edge makes work difficult and is potentially dangerous. More cut hands result from pushing too hard with a blunt chisel than from working with one with a well-sharpened blade.

Sharpening takes in both grinding and honing. Grinding is carried out on a revolving grindstone, which usually leaves a coarse finish unsuitable as a cutting edge. After grinding, tools then have to be honed, or whetted, usually on a sharpening stone – either an oil-stone or a water-stone – to produce a sharp cutting edge. In normal use, tools can be honed several times before regrinding becomes necessary.

Many grindstones are electrically driven, and most have narrow abrasive wheels revolving at about 3,000rpm (revolutions per minute) and are used dry. The danger here is that the steel being sharpened may overheat, and become soft as a result. The only way to keep this from happening is to dip the metal constantly in water to cool it. Machines with wider wheels revolving at only about 150-200rpm are more suitable.

Sharpening stones, usually oil-stones, come in three grades – coarse, medium, and fine – with the medium and fine grade generally being the most useful. Both natural and artificial stones are available. You should protect all types of oil-stone in a wooden box when they are not in use, and make sure that the surface is always lubricated with thin oil. The oil reduces the friction and floats off the fine metal residue produced by the sharpening process, which would otherwise clog the pores of the stone, causing the surface to glaze and become ineffective. Some stones use water as a lubricant. These stones are rather soft and easily damaged, but they do produce a fine edge. For really good results, the surface of your sharpening stone must be perfectly flat, so remember always to use the full width of the stone when sharpening tools.

When you buy new edge-cutting tools, such as planes and chisels, the blades supplied are ground but not honed. In order to hone a blade at the correct angle, hold it in both hands and place the ground bevel (which is about 25°) flat on the surface of the stone. Then raise your hands slightly to give an angle of about 30°, which is about right. Using moderate pressure, rub the blade back and forth along the full length of the stone's surface. This produces a fine burr, or wire edge, on the back of the blade (you can easily feel it with your thumb). Turn the blade over and, keeping it absolutely flat on the stone, rub the burr away to produce a sharp cutting edge. Check your results by holding the blade, edge up, to the light. Any bluntness will reflect light and show as a white line. For a superior cutting edge, strop the blade on a piece of leather dressed with oil and a mild abrasive.

One of the problems many beginners experience when honing is rocking the tool or blade. This rounds the bevel over and stops it from cutting properly. Maintaining the blade at the correct angle to the stone throughout the process can also cause problems. Gripping the blade firmly and keeping your wrists stiff help to combat the first problem, while a useful aid for both is the honing guide. This device runs on rollers and holds the blade firmly at precisely the correct honing angle to the stone while you push it back and forth.

WORKING METHODS

JOINING WOOD

There are numerous ways of joining pieces of wood together. Some involve metal fastenings, such as nails or screws, or use wooden dowels, while some rely entirely on the adhesion of glued surfaces or a combination of these methods. In others, the wooden components themselves are shaped into interlocking joints, such as mortise and tenons, dovetails, and so on, which form, when glued, permanent constructions.

These joining techniques have evolved slowly over centuries, and few of them can be improved. In recent times, however, the increased use of man-made, composite materials – plywood, blockboard, and MDF (medium-density fiberboard), for example – and the requirements of ease and speed of manufacture and assembly have resulted in the introduction of other methods of fastening and joining, such as the so-called knock-down fittings and other instant-joining systems. Here, however, the emphasis is on the use of solid, seasoned wood and the traditional methods of jointing, and only those techniques required to make the projects will be included.

Using nails Nails are available in a wide variety of types and sizes. The selection illustrated here includes those required in the projects. Nails are made of a variety of materials, including steel, galvanized steel, brass, copper, and aluminum, and are known generally as common nails, round and oval, and brads or finishing nails. Steel nails are suitable for most jobs – oval types reduce the risk of the wood splitting and you can set them below the surface for a neat finish. For light work, and in some furniture making, brads or finishing nails are more suitable; these too can be set below the surface of your work to make a hidden fixing.

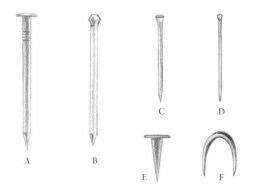

(A) Round wire nail (B) Oval nail (C) Lost head nail (D) Finishing nail (E) Tack or stud (F) Staple

Always use a nail or brad of suitable length. Long nails tend to bend easily, so support them between your index finger and thumb and take care when knocking them in. Short nails may be difficult to hold, especially if you have big hands, so try pushing them through a piece of cardboard held between your finger and thumb.

Nails used in conjunction with glue can make quite a strong joint. Strength is improved, especially on wide boards, if "dovetail nailing" is used. To make any nailed assembly easier, tap the nail or brad almost through the top piece first, apply the glue, and then position the pieces of wood together and knock the nail or brad all the way in. When working with hardwoods, which tend to split easily, it is best to predrill holes slightly smaller than the nails or brads to be used. For a neat finish, set the nails or brads below the surface of the wood using a small nail set and hammer. The nail set should have a concave tip to prevent it from

slipping off the nail head. Fill the holes left on the surface with wood putty or with a mixture of glue and sawdust.

Using screws Screws are used for joining pieces of wood together and for attaching hardware such as hinges, handles, and so on.

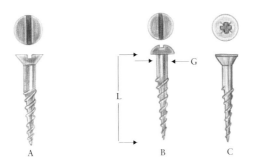

They are classified by length (L), gauge (G) (diameter of the shank), and type of head. They are made in steel or brass and there are also several steel-coated varieties, such as chromium and zinc. The size is specified by length and the gauge by a number – the larger the number, the thicker the screw. Head types are basically either countersunk or flat head (A) (designed to go flush with or below the surface of the wood) or round head (B) (designed to sit on the surface). Screws may have the traditional straight slot for use with a conventional screwdriver, or be cross-headed (C) for use with an appropriate screwdriver.

For most work in the projects section, countersunk, slotted steel screws are used. However, with oak you must always use brass screws to prevent the tannin in the wood from corroding the screws.

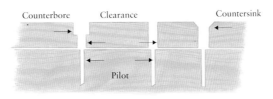

Drilled holes are necessary when joining wood with screws, and when attaching hardware. With hardwoods, drill a clearance hole – one fractionally larger than the screw diameter – through the top piece, and a pilot hole – one smaller than the diameter of the screw threads – to the full length of the screw. In softwoods, the top clearance hole

should be drilled, but you can use an awl for making the pilot hole. Use a countersink to recess the surface or counterbore the top and fill the surface with a wooden plug if you intend to conceal the head completely. Make sure you use the correct size of screwdriver for the size of screw, and press down firmly on the screw head as it is turned to prevent damage to the slot.

Using adhesives Using an appropriate adhesive is often the most satisfactory way to join wood to wood, especially when it is used with one of the interlocking types of joint or when reinforced by nails or screws. For the glue to have maximum strength, you must first clean the parts that are to come into contact to remove any dust or loose wood that could create gaps – don't use glue as a space filler if you want a good joint. Then you must keep the pieces in tight contact until the glue is properly dry (see the manufacturer's recommendations), usually by clamping them together.

Plan the gluing-up stage of your work carefully. Have a clear, dust-free area in which to work and first of all test fit the pieces together (without using glue) to make sure that everything fits properly and is square. Have your glue and a damp cloth on hand; clamps should be ready and set to the right size, with protective blocks available if needed. Use enough glue to prevent a dry joint but not so much that you create a messy clean-up job afterward. Wipe away any surplus glue with a damp cloth. Bear in mind that glue marks can mar the appearance of some surface finishes.

MAKING JOINTS

Edge jointing When a wide piece of wood is called for, it may be necessary to join two narrower pieces together, edge to edge. The simplest and most satisfactory method is to use the plain rubbed joint. For this to work, you need to make sure that the mating edges are true and square along their entire length. You can avoid the common error of planing more off the ends by planing the middle fractionally hollow. Planing the two edges at the same time helps guarantee accuracy. To test your results, hold the edges together and up to the light to identify any gaps.

When you are satisfied, apply glue to one of the adjoining edges, press the edges together, and rub them back and forth a few times. This removes any air from the joint and rubs the glue into the fibers – which gives the joint its name.

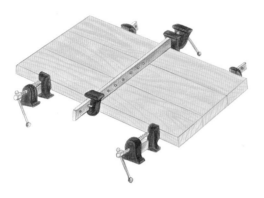

To hold the edges in tight contact, a minimum of three bar clamps are needed, placed as shown. Tighten the middle one first. Check your work for flatness, clean off any surplus glue, and leave it to dry overnight. Plane or, preferably, scrape the joint area clean if necessary afterward.

The plain rubbed joint is fine for most work, but for larger surfaces, such as table tops, you can use a similar joint strengthened with dowels or by a loose tongue. To make a wider board, purchased tongue-and-groove boards can be glued together.

Grooves and rabbets Although not strictly joints by themselves, grooves and rabbets form parts of joints. A groove is a narrow channel cut usually along the length of a component, and a rabbet is a recess along an edge, either with or across the grain. Both may be used to hold panels in place. Special-purpose all-metal planes are available for making grooves and rabbets. A rabbet plane will only cut a rabbet, while a router plane will tackle rabbets and grooves. There are various multiplanes that will also do both, and other work besides. When using these planes, make short cuts beginning at the far end of the work and finish off with light continuous cuts.

The portable electric router, fitted with interchangeable cutters, has now taken over the work once performed by these different hand tools. When it is used with a suitable guide fence or with a manufactured or custom-built routing table, the portable router is safe, accurate, and quick.

Dado This type of joint consists of a narrow trench or wide groove cut across the grain of a piece of wood into which the end of another piece, such as a shelf, is fitted. Dadoes may be full thickness (of the shelf) or bare-faced, meaning that the shelf thickness is reduced to fit a narrower dado, and they can be either made through or stopped, as shown. You can cut the joint entirely by hand, with a little help from a drilling machine if you like (see diagram above, right), or you can use an electric router.

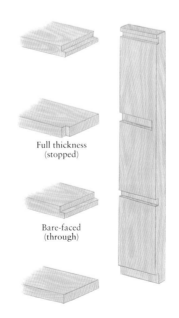

Full thickness (stopped)

Bare-faced (through)

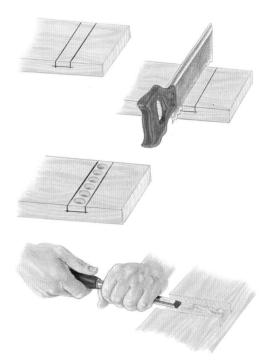

Begin by measuring the thickness of the shelf (or the bare-faced tongue made on the end of the shelf) and set out the position of the shelves on the supporting side pieces. Make the width of the dado joints fractionally less than the thickness of the shelves to ensure a tight fit. After checking, mark the cutting lines across the grain with a sharp marking knife. Gauge the depth of the joint – which is usually a third of the thickness of the side piece – from the inside face. Securely clamp the work to the bench. Using a sharp ¼-inch chisel, cut into the knifed lines on the waste side to form a guide groove for the saw. Saw down to the depth of the dado joint and then chisel out the waste wood, working in toward the center of the piece from both ends where possible. You can also use a drill to remove the bulk of the waste wood from the joint. Smooth the bottom of the joint and try the shelf for fit. If necessary, plane a shaving off the underside of the shelf until you get a tight fit.

Where one piece of wood meets another at a corner, as, for example, in a box construction, you can use similar dado joints. If the dado is full thickness, it becomes, in effect, a cross-grain rabbet, and you should secure it with glue and nails. However, a bare-faced housing is preferable in most circumstances, and if well made, this joint is strong enough using glue alone.

Dovetail joints You can get a much stronger corner joint using a dovetail joint, which is also particularly good for drawers. The strength of this joint lies in the increased gluing area and the interlocking shapes.

There are several types of dovetail, the simplest being the through dovetail where the end-grain portions of the joint, the tails and pins (the bits in between the tail sockets), are visible on both sides. In the lapped dovetail, often used on drawer fronts, the end grain is concealed on one face.

In drawer construction, you always cut the tails on the side pieces. Cut the materials to the required length and square across the end. Number, or otherwise identify, the mating ends. For through dovetails – that is, where the front and sides are the same thickness, mark out and cut the components as follows:

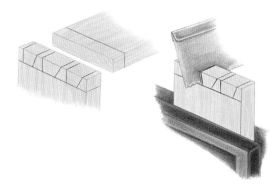

1. Set a marking (or cutting) gauge to the thickness of the wood and mark the ends of each piece all around – this is the depth line of the joint. Mark out the tails first, using either a T-bevel or a dovetail template. The tails should be evenly spaced and the marked positions squared across the end.

2. With the wood held upright in a vise, carefully saw on the waste side, using a dovetail or some other type of back saw, down to the depth line as shown above.

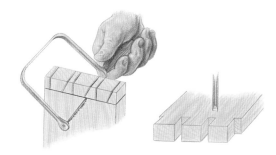

3. Remove the bulk of the waste wood using a coping saw and then finish removing the waste material from both sides with a sharp bevel-edge chisel.

4. Mark the sockets using the mating tails as a template. Hold the component to be marked upright in a vise and support the tail piece on it as shown. Align the tails carefully and mark clearly with a knife and square lines down to the depth line.

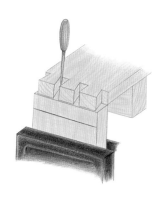

5. Cut away the waste wood as before, remembering to cut on the waste side of the marked lines, and clean out the joint with a sharp chisel. Test fit the joint and adjust as necessary with a chisel.

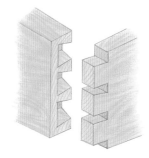

For lapped dovetails, the front piece is usually thicker than the sides – this extra thickness forms the lap that conceals the tails. Prepare your materials as described for through dovetails and, after deciding on the length of the tails (which are often equal to the thickness of the sides for convenience), set a marking gauge and mark the ends of the side pieces all around. Mark the front piece along the end and on the inside surfaces. Cut the tails and mark out the sockets as described for the through dovetail.

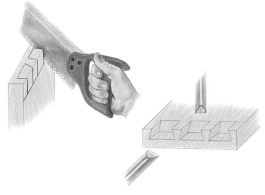

1. With the front piece held upright in a vise, carefully saw at an angle down to the gauged lines on the inside surface and lap. Remember to cut on the waste side of the lines.

2. With the piece secured flat on the bench, chisel out the waste wood beginning with vertical cuts (across the grain) and horizontal cuts. Use a sharp bevel-edge chisel and get right into the corners of the sockets. Test fit the joint and adjust as necessary.

You can cut dovetails by machine and these are usually recognizable by the even size and spacing of the pins and tails. Modern jigs, however, allow you to use a router to cut dovetails that are indistinguishable from hand-cut joints.

Cross-lapped joint Where two pieces of wood (usually of the same thickness) are to cross each other at right angles, and you want the surfaces to remain flush, you will have to use a cross-lapped joint, as shown in the diagram below.

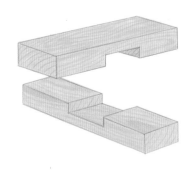

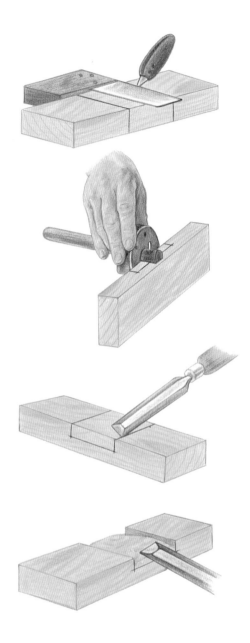

Although there are many variations of this joint, only three are considered here: the stub, or blind, mortise and tenon; the haunched mortise and tenon; and the more specialized double mortise and tenon. The main parts of each of these joints are the mortise, which is a recess or slot cut into (usually) the upright member or stile, and the tenon, which is a reduced projection on the end of the mating piece (generally called the rail) made to fit tightly into the mortise.

Plane materials true and square, making sure that they are square across the ends. Where mortises come close to the end, it is usual practice to leave some extra length to the stiles initially to prevent the wood splitting. These projections are sawn off later.

1. Cut the rails to length, remembering to allow for the length of both tenons. Mark the required rail length and square all around with a sharp knife. This is the shoulder line of the tenon.

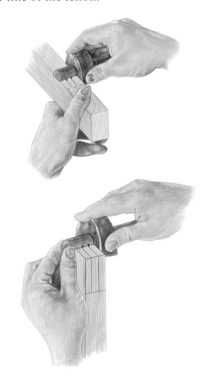

2. Mark the positions of the mortises. The width required is the width of the tenons. Set the spurs of a marking gauge to a chisel-width equal or close to a third of the thickness of the rail. Use the gauge at this setting to mark the thickness of the tenon all around and also to complete the marking of the mortise.

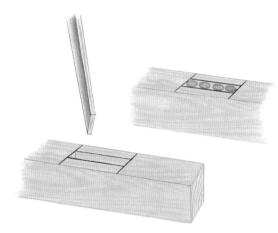

3. Cut the mortises first. If you are doing this by hand, it helps to drill vertically down between the marked lines with a smaller-sized drill to remove the bulk of the waste wood, and then use a chisel to clean and square the joint. Make mortises ⅛ inch deeper than the length of the tenon.

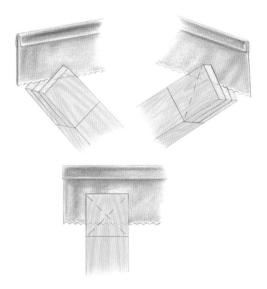

4. Now cut the tenons. With the rail held in a vise, saw down both cheeks to the shoulder line, cutting on the waste side of the marked lines, with a tenon saw in three stages, as shown above. Then, with the rail clamped to the bench, chisel a sloping groove into the knifed shoulder line, on the waste side, to

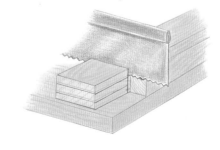

Plane the materials to size and square and mark the position of the joint full width and square across each piece using a sharp knife. Also mark the lines squared down the sides in pencil. Set a marking gauge to half the thickness of the wood and mark the depth of the joint equally on both pieces. Chisel a sloping groove into the knifed lines (on the waste side) to make a guide for the saw, and then saw vertically down to the gauged line indicating the depth of the joint. Chisel out the waste wood, working from both sides in toward the middle, and finish off the joint so that it is smooth and flat.

Mortise and tenon joints The strongest, as well as the most commonly used, type of framing joint is the mortise and tenon.

make a guide for the saw. Saw vertically down to the previously made saw cut to remove the cheek waste. Finally, mark the reduction in tenon width and saw off the waste (previous page).

5. Trim the tenon to a good fit in the mortise. Aim to keep everything square so that the joints don't cause the frame to twist.

The haunched mortise and tenon is ideal when making a frame that is grooved to accept a panel, as in a door. The haunch can help to strengthen the joint but here it also fits and fills the exposed end of the groove in the stile. Where possible, make the groove the same size as the mortise and cut out the mortise as previously described, after first cutting the groove. (See page 142.)

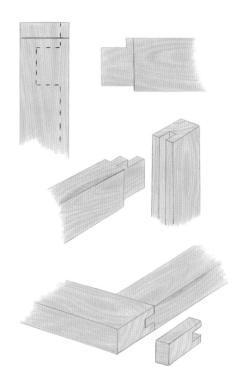

Mark the tenon and saw down the cheeks, but mark off and retain the haunch portion when sawing off the remaining waste. Trim to fit.

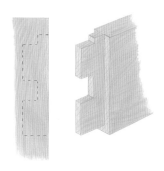

Double tenons are used when joining wide rails to stiles where the long mortise required for a single, wide tenon would weaken the stile, or where a wide tenon might become loose through shrinkage. It is, for example, the correct joint to use when jointing large paneled doors and deep apron table frames. Mark the joint as shown above. Cut the mortise, including the recess for the tenon haunch and central tongue, first. Then mark out and cut the double tenon, haunch, and tongue. Trim to fit.

There are machines for cutting mortises, as well as attachments that you can fit to a drill press to do the same. Tenoning machines are used in commercial manufacture, but on a smaller scale, by using suitable jigs, you can cut tenons on a circular saw or band saw, or with a router.

Round tenons into drilled sockets This is the traditional joint often used in stool and chair making to join legs to seats or cross rails to uprights. Sockets can be either bored "through" or "blind;" through joints are often wedged (see below). Some woodworkers advocate tapered sockets, but straight, parallel-sided sockets give a more secure joint. First, bore out the required size of

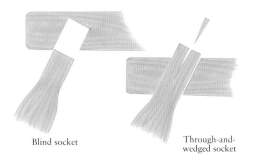

Blind socket   Through-and-
                      wedged socket

socket using a drill bit – the saw-toothed Forstner bit is most suitable – and then make the round tenon by whittling with a knife or rounding with cutting or abrasive tools. A general rule of thumb is that the socket depth should not be less than the socket diameter.

Draw boring (pegging joints)   An old method of tightening up and securing mortise and tenon joints is to insert a wooden pin or peg through the joint. This is known as draw boring, and it is often incorrectly copied in some modern reproduction furniture by boring through the assembled joint and simply inserting a dowel.

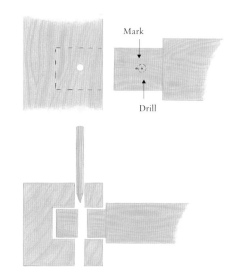

Mark

Drill

The correct way of making this joint is as follows. Cut the joint and withdraw the tenon. Then bore a suitable hole through the side of the mortise. Then replace the tenon to its full depth and insert the drill again to just mark the surface of the tenon inside the mortise. Withdraw the tenon, re-mark it about 1/16 inch nearer to the shoulder and drill through at this point. The slight offset you have created will draw the joint up really tight when you drive the pin in. The pin should be straight grained, and its head should be slightly larger than the hole and tapered to a point to ease starting. Cut the pin off flush on completion.

FINISHING

Some woods are more durable than others, but all will benefit from some kind of applied finish. Some finishes are designed to protect the surface by sealing the pores of the wood. Others, such as opaque paint, are used to obliterate or disguise the surface, while transparent polishes and varnishes serve to enhance and highlight the natural features of the wood. Additionally, finishes used on furniture act to give some resistance to the wear and tear of everyday use and abuse. Furthermore, many surface finishes can be renewed as time, and fashion, dictate.

Today there is a bewildering variety of wood-finishing materials. In earlier times, however, while there were several paint formulations and some oils and waxes, there was far less choice. For the country woodworker, choice was further limited by both cost and availability.

The subject of finishes is a complex one and here it is possible to make only general comments. Your local paint dealer should be able to advise you, and always read the manufacturers' labels on products before making your choice.

PAINT

The painted furniture and artefacts of Ancient Egypt and the evidence of the use of color in medieval dwellings give us some clues to the early use of "paint." Locally available earth and vegetable pigments were used to color a suitable medium, such as water (to make limewash and distemper), or combinations of water and other ingredients, such as linseed oil and egg yolk (to make tempera). Linseed oil was also used to make oil paints.

Milk paint Limewash and distemper proved less suitable for use on wood than on walls, and egg tempera and oil paint are expensive and time-consuming to make. In due course, a compromise product was found – milk paint. Milk paint is made by mixing earth pigments with skimmed milk and a little lime. In the rural communities of North America in particular, where its inexpensive ingredients were readily available and easy to prepare, milk paint became extremely popular. In addition to being easy to apply, it dries to a durable, smooth, flat finish. Moreover, milk paint produces clear colors that mellow nicely with age.

You apply milk paint with a brush or sponge, and since it is water soluble, it is pleasant to use and dries quite quickly, becoming lighter in color as it does so. A second coat will increase the opacity of the finish. When the paint has dried, you can add a coat of clear lacquer, glaze, or wax to seal and darken the surface. Milk paint is an authentic "old" paint finish, and one that is also environmentally friendly. Modern water-soluble paints include a choice of acrylics and latex paints.

Oil paint Oil-based paints were originally a mix of linseed oil, pigment, and white lead, with turpentine as a solvent. In modern formulations, oil-based paint is more likely to be a blend of oils and synthetic resins, with the lead omitted for safety and health reasons. The usual solvent is mineral spirits. Available in a very wide range of colors and three different finishes – flat, satin, and gloss – these paints are totally opaque and provide a reasonably tough and durable surface finish. With bare wood, however, you first need to apply a primer or undercoat. The disadvantages of oil paint are that it is slow to dry and brushes and so on have to be cleaned in mineral spirits or turpentine.

VARNISHES

Traditional varnish is made from natural gums, such as copal, dissolved in oil (linseed) or spirit (denatured alcohol). This creates a product with a transparent, or near transparent, appearance that can be applied to prepared bare wood or over flat paint to act as a protective top coat. Varnish also acts as a preservative and as a means of obtaining a good, hard-wearing surface finish.

Today, the most common type of "varnish" is polyurethane, available in flat, satin, and gloss. Polyurethane gives a hard, durable finish and it also provides effective protection against moisture. It is best to brush on a number of thinned coats (diluted half and half by volume with mineral spirits) than one full-strength application straight from the can. Allow each coat to dry thoroughly and sand the surface of each coat (except the final top coat) with very fine sandpaper. Be meticulous about removing dust, though, or the surface finish will be marred.

STAINS

Wood stains alter or enrich the color of wood and enhance the natural figure, or grain pattern, of a piece of furniture. There are four general types: water stains, spirit stains, oil stains, and chemical stains. Never use any stain without first testing it.

Prepare the wood carefully before staining it. Surface blemishes and coarse grain will be emphasized by the stain, while patches of grease or adhesive will reject the treatment and leave an uneven finish.

Water stains penetrate the fibers of the wood, and cause the grain to rise, making it necessary to sand the wood smooth before proceeding. Wetting the wood with water, allowing it to dry, and then sanding before staining reduces this problem. Oil stains do not cause the grain to rise, but they are slow drying and relatively expensive. Spirit-based stains are probably the most difficult to apply evenly because of their rapid drying time – dark patches where the stain overlaps can be a problem. Chemical stains work by reacting with the wood, and the resulting color can be unpredictable. After applying any stain, and after it has thoroughly dried, seal the surface of the wood with varnish, oil, or wax.

WAX AND OIL

Beeswax and linseed oil are probably the oldest known surface finishes. Both are transparent, or nearly so, and both impart a wonderful luster that brings out the best qualities of color and grain of your wood. Readily available and quite easy to apply, both are popular and widely used. The disadvantages of both are that they offer comparatively little surface protection and are easily marred. But the virtue of these finishes is that they are easy to renew.

Wax There are several good polishes you can buy, but make sure the one you choose is based on beeswax – some use paraffin wax instead. Avoid polishes that contain silicon – these produce a much advertised "sparkle," but not much else in terms of protecting or nourishing the wood. All waxes are incompatible with other finishes.

You can apply wax polish to bare wood and progressively build up the surface you want with additional applications. However, by giving the wood an initial application of a sealer, such as sanding sealer or a thinned coat of shellac or polyurethane, the wax will be more evenly distributed and you will save yourself a lot of work. Sand the sealer with a very fine abrasive before waxing. Apply the wax with a soft cloth, rub it in well, and leave it to dry for a few minutes before buffing it with a clean, dry cloth. Subsequent applications of wax will improve the sheen and, in time, help to produce a rich patination.

Oil "Once a day for a week, once a week for a month, once a month for a year, and once a year forever" is an old adage about applying an oil finish. The traditional oil was linseed, and its use does indeed require numerous applications. Each must dry (by oxidization) before the next is applied, and the idea is to go on doing this until the wood can absorb no more oil.

Boiled linseed oil dries more quickly than the raw form, but modern formulations, such as teak, tung, and Danish oils incorporating rapid oxidizing agents, are now more commonly used. You apply these commercial oils in the same way as linseed, by brushing or on a cloth, but because they are more penetrating and quicker to dry, they require only two or three applications.

AGING

There are various techniques you can use to simulate the effects of age, sunlight, dust, damp, and the general wear and tear of years of use. Known generally as "distressing" or "antiquing," these methods are now widely practiced and accepted for their esthetic appeal, although they are also used by fakers trying to pass modern-built furniture off as genuinely old. Distressing can involve doing actual damage to the wood, as well as using special finishes to simulate fading, peeling, crazing, patination, and similar effects.

Distressing wood Before applying any finish, you can age wood artificially by denting or scratching it, by scrubbing its surface with a wire brush, and by rounding over or purposely chipping corners and edges. Softwoods such as pine are especially suited to the wire-brush method. Wear on chair rails, table legs, etc., can easily be simulated by abrading these surfaces, but for an authentic look make sure that you apply this artificially induced damage where it would occur in normal use.

A common method of further aging new wood is to wipe it over with an antiquing glaze, made by mixing together small amounts of pigment such as burnt umber, raw sienna, or Vandyke brown in a transparent oil glaze. Make a suitable glaze by mixing 1 part boiled linseed oil with 2 parts mineral spirits, or substitute thinned oil or polyurethane varnish. Alternatively, you can use a water-based glaze. Simply wipe or brush on this tinted glaze and then immediately wipe it off again, leaving some pigment behind in the dents, hollows, crevices, and cracks of the wood.

Thinned gray or cream flat-finish paint brushed on and wiped off again will leave enough pigment behind in the grain of hardwoods to simulate age or a limewashed effect. Commercially produced "old pine" stain will also age softwoods convincingly. Formulations containing lime, caustic soda or lye, ammonia, or sulfuric acid can also be effective, but they are dangerous to use and you need to take extreme care.

Antique waxes – wax polish containing darkening pigments – applied to new wood will quickly give the appearance of a build-up of polish and dirt, which is what gives the patina of age. You can buy suitable wax polishes already tinted or make them yourself by adding pigments or shoe polish to ordinary wax furniture polish.

Distressing paint You can also apply antiquing glaze over a painted surface. This will darken the color of the paint, producing an effect that would naturally take years to achieve. Rubbing a painted surface with abrasive paper or steel wool will lighten its color, simulating both wear and tear and the effects of exposure to sunlight. Abrading the surface color right off in places will allow underlying paint colors to show through in those areas. This can be a very effective technique, but you can also try applying a first coat of paint and allowing it to dry before applying a second one in a contrasting color. Before this second coat has dried, rub it off in the areas that would normally receive the most wear to reveal the color beneath (and perhaps, too, some areas of bare wood as well). It is very helpful to examine a real antique painted piece first to give you some ideas of how the end result should look.

Flaking paint is often a characteristic associated with old furniture, especially items that have been exposed to damp. Applying patches of wax, either to bare wood or a previously painted surface, will stop additional coats of paint adhering to those patches. When the top coat is dry, gently rub back the previously waxed areas to cause the paint to flake. Dampness may also cause painted surfaces to crack and craze. You can simulate this by using special "crackle" varnishes. This process makes use of the incompatibility and different drying times of oil-based and water-based varnishes. The best effects are achieved when two coats of contrasting base paints are used. If required, you can wipe more color into the cracked surface after it has dried.

All distressing and antiquing processes require careful, restrained application if they are to be convincing. Bear in mind that wear would occur in some areas more than others, and that dust and dirt would tend to accumulate in recesses such as deep moldings. Also bear in mind that exposed surfaces, such as sharp edges, table tops, and drawer fronts, would tend to be lighter in color due to normal wear and the fading effects of sunlight. Around door and drawer pulls, you would also normally find signs of wear and tear and a build-up of grime. Use artists' colors applied with a small brush to produce the desired effect.

Once you have achieved an aged appearance, apply a protective coat of varnish – but don't let it get too shiny.

WOOD GUIDE

It helps to know something of a wood's characteristics – its working properties, color, durability, and so on – before choosing a particular type for a specific project. It also helps to know if it is botanically a hardwood (H) or a softwood (S). Below, you will find a brief guide to those North American and European timbers that have been used or recommended for the projects in this book and that are easily available to the country woodworker.

You can readily purchase prepared wood from lumber yards and other types of retail outlets (see Directory, pages 156-7). Softwoods are generally less expensive to buy than hardwoods. In some countries, large quantities of wood – both hardwoods and softwoods – are sold by volume, i.e. by the cubic foot. This is a quantity of wood equal to a board 1in thick x 12in wide x 12ft long. For smaller amounts, it is more usual to be quoted a price per piece or per foot (meter) for a given, measured section. The standard measurement in America is the board foot, which is equal to a wooden board 1in thick x 12in square.

Ash (H)
The European ash (*Fraxinus excelsior*) is a large tree whose common name generally reflects its country of origin. In Canada and the United States, the ash (*F. americana*) is generally a little smaller than its European counterpart, but there are many varieties – such as black, white, yellow, and blue ash. It has a coarse but usually straight grain and is characterized by its strength and resilience. It is whitish to light brown in color, has a distinctive figure (grain pattern), is easy to work, and takes a good polish. It is not durable outdoors, however, unless it is treated with a preservative.

Beech (H)
This strong, hardwearing wood has many good properties from the woodworker's point of view. The European beech (*Fagus sylvatica*) grows into a large tree and is favored for the fine, uniform texture of its wood. The American beech (*F. grandifolia*) is a relatively small tree but with similar strength and working properties to its European counterpart, although it does have a slightly coarser texture. Beech is generally pale to reddish brown in coloration, and although its grain pattern often lacks real character, it stains and polishes to a good finish. Beech requires treatment with a preservative if you intend to use it in damp conditions.

Birch (H)
This is probably the world's hardiest and most-widespread tree. Birch (*Betula sp.*) varies from invasive scrub to moderate-sized trees. The characteristic birch of North America is the paper birch (*B. papyrifera*), while sweet birch (*B. lenta*) and yellow birch (*B. alleghanensis*) are also common. In Britain, the silver birch (*B. pendula*) and *B. pubescens* are common types. Birch has a creamy white sap wood and pale brown heartwood. It works and finishes reasonably well, but it is not durable when used outdoors.

Cedar (S)
The true cedar, cedar of Lebanon (*Cedrus libani*), is a large tree with a trunk up to 5ft in diameter. Its wood is straight grained, if a little brittle, but it is easy to work (except around any knots). The cedar has an aromatic wood whose scent is known to discourage moths. American "cedars" include white cedar (*Thuja occidentalis*), western red cedar (*T. plicata*), yellow cedar (*Chamaecyparis nootkatensis*), and others. Both the white and western red cedars are reddish brown in coloration and slightly coarse grained, and western red cedar splits easily. Yellow cedar is fine textured, easily worked, and pale yellow in color.

Cherry (H)
American cherry, also known as black cherry (*Prunus serotina*), is a good, decorative wood, fine textured and straight grained. It makes a tree of moderate size, although there are smaller varieties such as the pin and sweet cherries. The European cherry (*P. avium*) is also a small tree and its wood is mainly used only for small-scale work. Cherry wood, which is reddish brown in color, is not difficult to work if your tools are sharp. It finishes well and takes a high polish.

Elm (H)
Once common in parts of North America and Britain, elm – including *Ulmus americana* and *U. procera*, the American and English elms, respectively – is fast disappearing due to the ravages of Dutch elm disease. Larger in size in Britain than in America, elm trees produce wood that is coarse textured and often cross grained, but it works well if your tools are sharp. Its color is beige-brown and most varieties and hybrids have an attractive figure, especially *U. procera*. It is not naturally durable when used outdoors.

Hazel (H)

More of a shrub than a tree, the European hazel (*Corylus avellana*) is widespread throughout much of Britain, where, in the past, it was extensively grown as coppice. It produces strong, straight, pliable sticks for a variety of craft applications. Native American hazels include *C. americana* and *C. californica*.

Hickory (H)

Native to Canada and eastern parts of America, hickory (*Carya glabra* and *C. laciniosa*, among others) is a strong, straight-grained wood similar in appearance and main characteristics to ash. Its fiberous wood is tougher than that of ash, however.

Lime (H)

A fine-textured wood, lime (*Tilia vulgaris*), which is also known as linden, is easily worked and, because it cuts evenly in all directions, it is excellent when you need a wood for carving. Lime has a creamy white-colored wood. The American lime (*T. americana*) is known as Basswood – the name that is also given to the wood of the tulip tree.

Maple (H)

Of the many maples, sugar maple (*Acer saccharum*), also known as hard or rock maple, is perhaps best known throughout North America. It is a heavy, hard wood with a close-textured grain, white to pale brown in color. It can sometimes be difficult to work, but it is hard wearing and finishes well. Red maple (*A. rubrum*) is not as hard or strong as *Acer saccharum*, but it is easier to work. In Britain, the field maple (*A. campestre*) is generally little more than a small hedgerow tree of limited commercial value. None of the maples is naturally durable when used outdoors.

Oak (H)

There are many different types of oak. American varieties are generally known as white oak (*Quercus alba*) and red oak (*Q. rubra*), while the two varieties native to Britain are the common, or European, oak (*Q. robur*) and the sessile oak (*Q. petraea*). Oak wood is renowned for its strength and durability, but these qualities vary according to growing conditions and growth rates. All are hard and durable and work well. White oak has similar characteristics to the European varieties, while red oak is coarser grained and has a less attractive figure. Color varies from pale yellow to brown, often with a pinkish tint. Oak wood contains tannic acid, which corrodes ferrous metals.

Pine (S)

This wood is used more than any other around the world. Pine is the common name given to all members of the *Pinus* family – and, commercially, to several others that are not. The character of the 35 or so varieties of American pine varies geographically from the hard, pitch pines of the south (*P. palustris*) to the softer pines such as Weymouth or yellow pine (*P. strobus*) of the east and the western white pine (*P. monticola*). Yellow pine is an easily worked wood, pale yellow to brown in color, while western white pine is similar but tougher. In Europe, Scots pine (*P. sylvestris*), especially, provides the popular red deal or redwood, which is a relatively strong, slightly resinous wood, yellow-brown to red-brown in color, often with a distinctive figure. It works easily and well (except around the knots), and can be brought to a good finish. All the varieties of pines take stain, paint, and polish well. None is durable outdoors, however, unless first treated with preservatives.

Sycamore (H)

American and British sycamores are unrelated trees – the former belong to the plane family (*Platanus occidentalis*), while the latter are maples (*Acer pseudoplatanus*), the false plane. The American sycamore is an even-textured wood, pale reddish brown in color, and is easy to work and polishes well. The British sycamore also has an even texture but it is finer textured and is white to creamy white in color. It works and finishes well, coming to a lustrous surface. Neither species is durable if used outdoors.

Walnut (H)

This is a fine, distinctive wood with some excellent woodworking characteristics. American black walnut (*Juglans nigra*) grows to be a large tree. It has a tough, rather coarse-textured wood, with both straight and wavy grain. Its heartwood is rich purple brown to black in color. It works well, takes a high polish, and is moderately durable when used outdoors. European walnut (*J. regia*) is a smaller tree, and its wood varies in color from gray brown to brown, often with darker streaks evident. Its characteristics and working properties are similar to *J. nigra*.

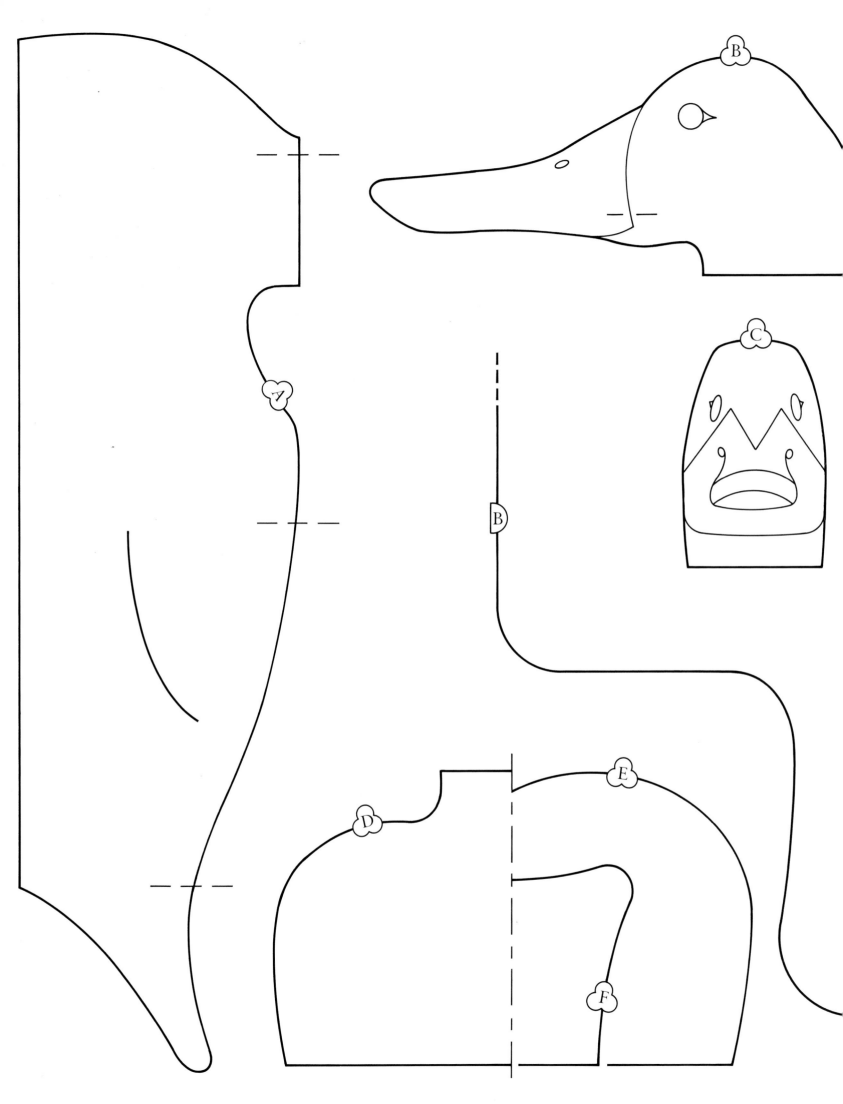

TEMPLATES

The template patterns on pages 150–5 have been grouped together by design project (see key). To save space, the patterns overlap, but you can easily differentiate between the pieces by looking for the identifying letters found inside a coded bubble along one of the edges. Make a separate tracing for each pattern piece, making sure that you label each one with the appropriate letter. The templates on pages 150–4 are full size; those on page 155 have been reduced in size with each grid square representing 1 inch.

♡ **Duck Decoy** 6 *patterns (A–F) page 150*

▽ **Cutting Boards** 2 *patterns (B, C) pages 150, 151*

▽ **Spoon Rack** 2 *patterns (A, B) page 151*

♡ **Candle Box** 3 *patterns (A–C) page 152*

◇ **Five-Board Bench** 1 *pattern (A) page 152*

⬠ **Hooded Cradle** 2 *patterns (A, B) page 153*

□ **Folk Bed** 1 *pattern (A) page 153*

○ **Traditional Whirligig** 8 *patterns (A–H) page 154*

◇ **Rocking Chair** 5 *patterns (A–E) page 155*

⬭ **Shaker Shelves** 1 *pattern (A) page 155*

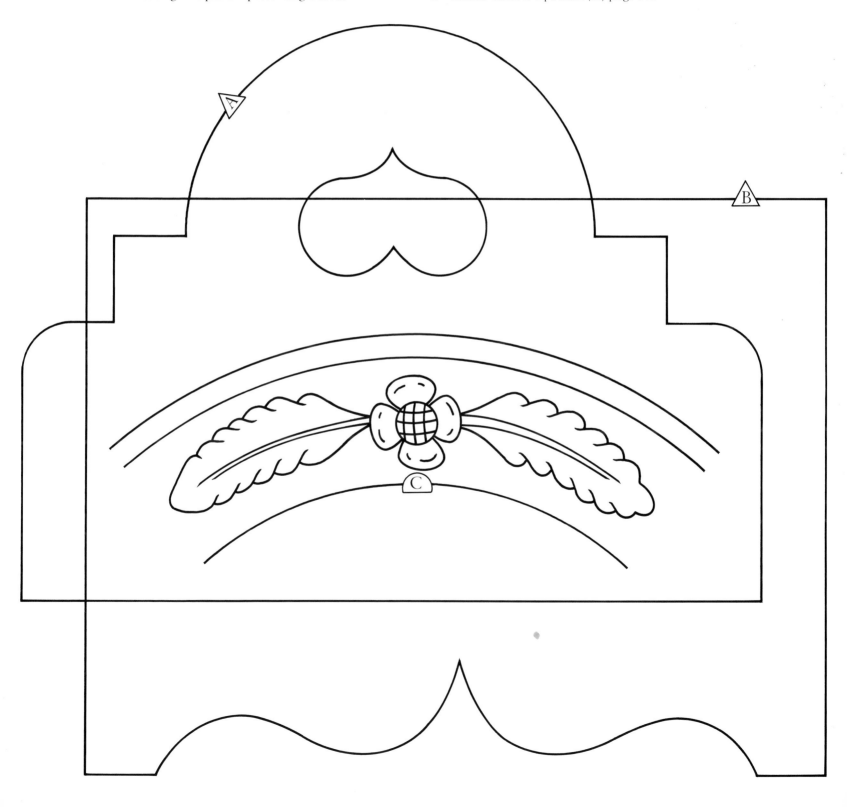

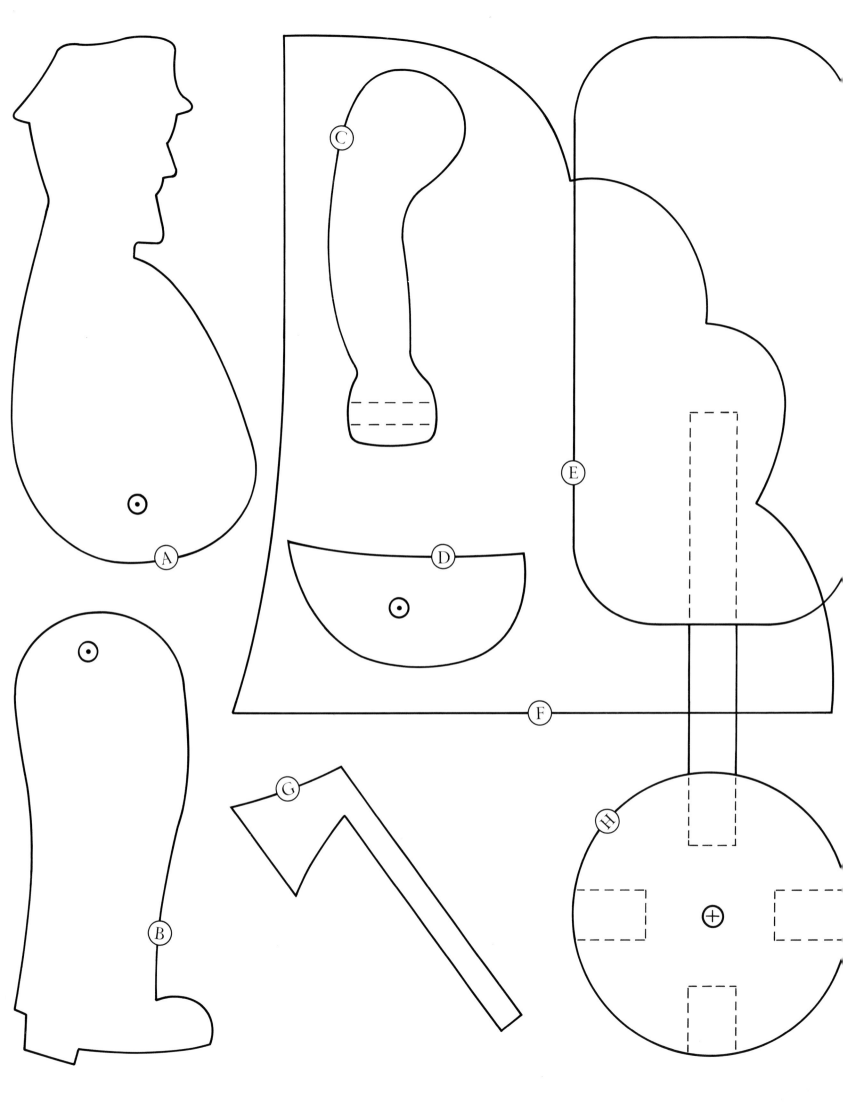

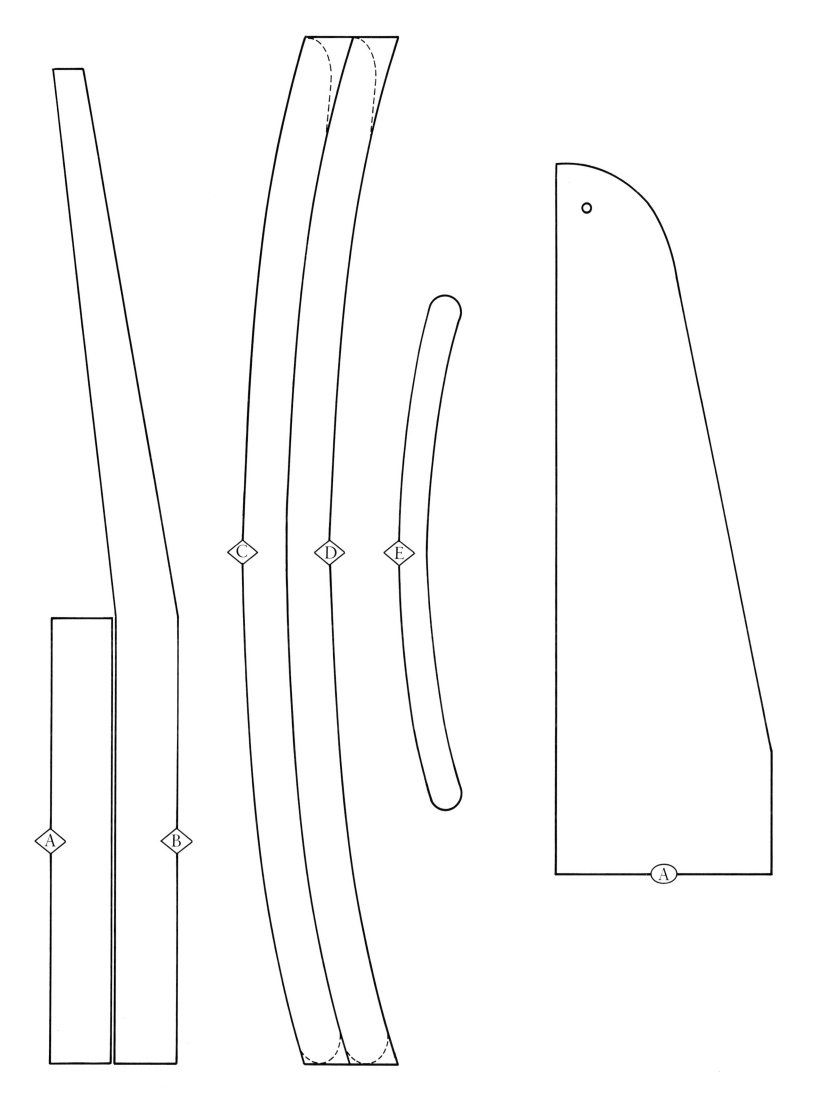

DIRECTORY OF SUPPLIERS

WOOD AND TOOLS

Colonial Hardwoods Inc.
7953 Cameron Brown Ct
Springfield, VA 22153
Domestic hardwoods.

Constanine
2050 Eastchester Road
DPT 37501
Bronx, NY 10461
Wood, tools, accessories,
finishing supplies.

Craft Supplies USA
PO Box 50300
Provo, UT 84605-0030
Tools, accessories.

Garratt Wade Co. Inc.
161 Avenue of the Americas
New York, NY 10313
Tools, accessories, finishing
supplies.

Handloggers
135 E. Sir Francis Drake Bvd
Larkspur, CA 94939
Domestic & sustainable source
hardwoods.

Peter Lang Co.
3115 Porter Creek Road
Santa Rosa, CA 95404
Domestic hardwoods &
softwoods.

Talarico Hardwoods
Route 3, Box 3268
Mohnton, PA 19540-9939
Domestic hardwoods.

Willard Brothers
300 Basin Road
Trenton, NJ 08619
Domestic hardwoods.

Woodcraft
210 Wood County Industrial
Park
PO Box 1686
Parkersburg, WV 26101-1686
Wood, tools, accessories.

Woodcrafters Supply
2920 Buffalo Road
Erie, PA 16510
Domestic & imported wood,
tools, books.

PAINTS AND FINISHES

Antique Color Supply Inc.
PO Box 711
Cambridge, MA 01451
Milk paints, etc.

Flax's
1699 Market Street
San Francisco, CA 94103
Paint products.

Liberon
PO Box 86
Medocino, CA 95460
Wax polish, stains & other
finishing products.

Martin Senour Co.
101 Prospect Ave. NW
Cleveland, OH 44115
Paint products.

Waynes Woods Inc.
39 North Plains Industrial Road
Wallingford, CT 06492
Stains, finishing products.

MISCELLANEOUS

Ball & Ball
463 West Lincoln Highway
Exton, PA 19341
Furniture hardwood, locks,
hinges, etc.

Connecticut Cane & Reed
PO Box 762B
Manchester, CT 06040
Seat-weaving materials, Shaker
seating tape.

Paxton Hardware Ltd
PO Box 256
Upper Falls, MD 21156
Locks, hinges, etc.

Shaker Workshops
Box 1028
Concord, MA 01742
Shaker furniture, kits, seating
tape, etc.

PLACES OF INTEREST

BRITAIN

American Museum in Britain
Claverton Manor
Bath BA2 7BT
England
Colonial & Shaker interiors,
furniture & artefacts.

Highland Folk Museum
Duke Street
Kingussie
Inverness-shire PH21 1JG
Scotland
Early local furniture &
artefacts.

Museum of Lakeland Life &
Industry
Abbot Hall
Kendal LA9 5AL
England
Trade workshops & period
interiors, tools, etc.

Norfolk Rural Life Museum
Beech House
Grassenhall
East Dereham NR20 4DR
England
Labourers' cottage, furniture,
artefacts, tools, etc.

Welsh Folk Museum
St Fagins
Cardiff CF5 6XB
Wales
Furnished period cottages, rural
artefacts, tools.

NORTH AMERICA

Adirondack Museum
Blue Mountain Lake
New York, NY 12812
*History & crafts of the region,
rustic furniture.*

Colonial Williamsburg
PO Box C
Williamsburg, VA 23187
*Early Colonial interiors,
furniture & artefacts.*

Hancock Shaker Village
Albany Road
Route 20, PO Box 898
Pittsfield, MA 02102
*Shaker interiors, furniture,
artefacts, etc.*

Metropolitan Museum of Art
Fifth Avenue at 82nd Street
New York, NY 10028
*Rare, early furniture &
artefacts.*

Old Sturbridge Village
1 Old Sturbridge Village Road
Sturbridge, MA 01566
Colonial-period furniture.

WOODWORKING COURSES

Anderson Ranch
Box 5598
Snowmass, CO 81615
Country woodworking.

John C. Campbell
Folk School
Route 1
Box 14A
Brasstown, NC 28902-9603
Folk arts & crafts.

Country Workshops
90 Mill Creek Road
Marshall, NC 28753
*Country & green
woodworking.*

Dana Robes
Wood Craftsmen
Lower Shaker Village
Enfield, NH 03748
Shaker furniture & artefacts.

Warwick Country Workshops
PO Box 665
Warwick, NY 10990
Traditional woodworking.

Note: while every effort has
been made to ensure that the
above details are accurate and
up to date, these details may
vary from time to time.

BIBLIOGRAPHY

Gilborn, Craig. *Adirondack Furniture and the Rustic Tradition.*
Abrams Inc., New York. 1987.

Hill, Jack. *Country Chair Making.*
David & Charles, Newton Abbot. 1993.

Kettell, Russell H. *The Pine Furniture of Early New England.*
Dover, New York. 1949.

Kinmonth, Claudia. *Irish Country Furniture.*
Yale University Press. 1993.

Knell, David. *England Country Furniture.*
Berry & Jenkins, London. 1992.

Mack, Daniel. *Making Rustic Furniture.*
Sterling Lark, New York. 1992.

Miller, Judith & Martin. *Period Finishes and Effects.*
Mitchell Beazley, London. 1992.

Shea, John G. *Antique Country Furniture of North America.*
Van Nostrand Reinhold, New York. 1975.

Sparkes, Ivan. *English Domestic Furniture.*
Spurbooks, Bourne End. 1980.

Sprigg, J. & Larkin, D. *Shaker: Life, Work, and Art.*
Cassell, London. 1988.

INDEX

Page numbers in *italic* refer to pictures and captions; those in **bold** refer to projects.

A

abrasives *see* sandpaper
adhesives 140
  using 141
Adirondack-style furniture 18, *46*
  "twig" bed 106, *106*
Aga ranges 77
aging wood 147
Amish community:
  log house *46*
"antiquing" 147
armoires 19, 99
auger bits 139
aumbries 19, 99

B

back saws 137
band saws 137, 145
bar clamps 139
  using 142
bathroom furniture 115
bathtubs *115*
  boxing in 115
beading tools 119
bedding, storing
  see blanket boxes
bedrooms 106
  children's 113
  storage in 109–10
beds 106, 129
  Adirondack-style "twig" 106, *106*
  built-in 113, *113*
  children's *112*, 113
  four-poster *106*, 129
  pine *129*, **130–1**
  sleigh 106
  trundle 106, 113
  see also settle-beds
beeswax polishes 146, 147
bench dogs 136
benches (seats) *33*, 49, 55
  five-board 55, *55*, **56–7**
  kitchen *74*
  "monks'" 19, *49*
benches, work 136
bench-hooks 136
bench stops 136
bentwood chairs 65, *65*, 80

bird baths 50
bird cage *50*
bird houses
  see nesting boxes
bits, drill 139
  Forstner 139, 145
blanket boxes 109, 124, *124*, **126–7**
block planes 138
boards, cutting 83, 95, *95*, **96**, *96*
Boston Rocker, the 65
bowls, wooden 83, *83*
boxes 22
  blanket 109, 124, *124*, **126–7**
  bobbin 22
  candle 22, *22*, **24–5**, *25*
  dice and domino 22
  "keeping" 22
  knife *80*, 87, *113*
  nesting
    see nesting boxes
  round *83*, 84
  Shaker 84
  tobacco 22
  toy 113
  wall-mounted *see* cupboards, wall-hung
bradawls, using 139, 141
brad point bits 139
buckets, wooden 83, *83*, 84
butter mold *90*

C

cabinet scrapers 138
candle boxes 22, *22*, **24–5**, *25*
candles 34
candle stands 34, *34*, **36–7**
C clamps 136, 139
center bits 139
chairs 55, 80
  bentwood 65, *65*, 80
  double-comb back (Windsor) *31*
  ladderback *16*, 49, *49*, 80, *80*
  lath-back 49, *49*
  rocking 49, *49*, 65, *65*, **66–7**
  rustic 68, *68*, **70–1**
  Windsor *18*, 49, 80, *96*
  see also stools
chamfers, making 138

chests 109, 124
  see also blanket boxes
chests of drawers *106*, 109, *109*, 110
Chippendale-style sofa *16*
chisels 138, 139
  sharpening 140
  using 139, 142, 144
churn ladles 90, **93**
circular saws 137, 145
clamps 136, 139
  C 136
  sash/bar 139, 142
closets 110, *110*
  see also cupboards
clothes pegs *84*
compasses, using 137
containers, storage 83, *83*, 84
  see also boxes; cupboards *etc.*
coping saws 137
cots 113
  see also cradles
countersinking screws 139, 141
"crackle" varnishes 147
cradles 113, 121, *121*
  hooded 121, *121*, **122–3**
cribs 113
crosscut saws 137
cross-halving *or* cross-lapped joints 143–4
cupboards 19, 99
  livery 99
  New England style *18*
  painted 19, *19*
  pine *18*, 19, *19*, *21*, 78
  wall-hung *21*, 99, *99*, **100–2**
  see also dressers
curtain fabrics 16
cutlery *see* knives; spoons
cutters, half-moon *84*
cutting boards 83, 95, *95*, **96**, *96*
cutting gauges 137

D

dado joints 142
decoys, duck 31, *31*, **32–3**
dice boxes 22
dining rooms 74
  tables 77–8

dippers, wooden 90
"distressing" 147
  paint 147
  wood 147
dividers, using 137
domino boxes 22
door panels, jointing 145
dough bowls 83, *83*
dovetail joints 124, *124*, 137, 140, 143
"dovetail nailing" 141
dovetail saw 137
dowels:
  "blind" 33
  for edge jointing 142
draw boring (joints) 145–6
drawers, making **42**, **102**, 143
drawings and plans:
  orthographic 136
  perspective 136
drawknives 138
dressers 77, 80, *80*, 83, 99
  pine *18*
  pot-board 83
dressing tables 109
drilling 28–9, 139
  of large holes 52
drill presses 139
drills and drill bits 139
duck decoys 31, *31*, **32–3**

E

edge jointing 141–2
edges, planing 138, 141
electric tools
  see power tools

F

files 138, 139
finger gauging 137
finishes:
  oil 146, 147
  paint 146
  stains 146
  varnishes 146
  wax 146, 147
  see also "distressing"
fireplaces *16*, 18, 65
  kitchen 74, 77
flour scoops **92-3**
forms 55
  see also benches
Forstner bits 139, 145
French furniture 12, *110*

G

gardens:
  bird baths 50
  furniture 49, 68, *68*, **70–1**
  whirligigs 58, *58*, **60–2**
  see also nesting boxes
garnet paper 140
gate-leg tables 78
gauges:
  cutting 137
  mortise 137
  marking 137
gauging, finger 137
Gesner, Abraham 34
glasspaper 140
glazes, "antiquing" 147
glues 140
  using 141
gouges 138, 139
  sharpening 140
grinding tools 140
grindstones, electric 140
grooves, making 137, 138, 142

H

hammers, using 139, 141
hearths
  see fireplaces
heart shapes, cutting 24
Henry, O.: *Whirligigs* 58
honing tools 140
housing joints 142

I

"I" trestles 78

J

"Jack Chopping Wood" (whirligig) 58, **60–2**
jack planes 138
jig saws 134, 137
joints 140
  cross-halving *or* cross-lapped 143–4
  dado 142
  dovetail 124, *124*, 137, 140, 143
  draw boring (pegging) 145–6
  housing 142
  mortise and tenon 134, 140, 144–5
  rubbed (for edges) 141–2
  tenon and socket 145

K

"keeping" boxes
  see boxes, "keeping"
kerfs 136
kitchens 74, 77
  chairs 80
  dressers 80, 83
  tables 39, 77–8, 80
  utensils and containers
    25, 83–4, *84* (*see also*
    boxes; ladles; scoops;
    spoons *etc.*)
knife boxes 80, 87, *113*
knives:
  drawknives 138
  hooked 89
  marking 137

L

ladderback chairs *16*, 80,
  80
ladles 83, 90, *90*, **92**
  churn 90, **93**
  cordial *or* punch 90
  with spout 90, **93**
lath-back chairs 49, *49*
Lee, Ann 116
letter rack 22
linseed oil 146
  applying 147
livery cupboards 99
living-room furniture
  16–21
locks, fitting **127**
log house, Amish *46*
Loudon, John Claudius:
  Encyclopedia... 83
love spoons 87

M

mallets, using 139
marking gauges, using 137
marking knives, using 137
marking out 136, 137
measurements:
  making 136–7
  transferring 137
milk paint 21, 146
monks' benches 19, *49*
mortise and tenon joints
  134, 137, 140, 144–5
mortise gauges, using 137

N

nails 141, *141*
  using 139, 141
nesting boxes 50, *50*,
  52–3, *83*

New England style 12
  dresser *18*
  monk's bench *49*
nurseries 113

O

oak, screwing into 141
oil finishes 146, 147
oil paints 146
oil-stones 140
orthographic drawings 136
ovens 77

P

pails *see* buckets
paint 146
  "distressing" 147
  milk 21, 146
  oil-based 146
paneling, wood *33*, 115, *115*
  for bathtubs 115
panel pins *141*
  using 141
pegboards (Shaker) 116, *116*,
  119
pegging (of joints) 145–6
  see also dowels
pegs, clothes *84*
Pembroke tables 78
Pennsylvania style 12, 106,
  109, *110*
perspective drawings 136
pincers, using 139
pins, panel *141*
  using 141
pipe boxes 22
pit-sawing 78
planes:
  bench 137
  electric 138
  grooving 137, 138
  jack 138
  plough 142
  rabbet 142
  sharpening 140
  smoothing 138
planing 138
  of edges 141
plans *see* drawings
plate rack 77
platters, wooden 83
plough planes 142
polishes, wax 146, 147
polyurethane finishes 146
power tools 134
  drills 139
  grindstones 140
  mortise machines 145

planers 138
  routers 138, 142, 145
  sanders 139, 140
  saws 137, 145
  tenoning machines 145
punching nails 139, 141

R

rabbets, making 142
racks:
  plate 77
  spoon 87, *87*, **88–9**
ranges 77
rasps 138, 139
rip saws 137
rocking chairs 49, *49*, 65, *65*,
  66–7
rocking horses 113
rolling pins 83
routers, electric 138, 141,
  145

S

saber saws 137
sanders, electric 139, 140
sandpaper 140
  using 140
sash clamps 139
  using 142
sawbuck tables 78
sawing 136, 137
saws:
  back 137
  band 137, 145
  bow 137
  circular 137, 145
  coping 137
  cross-cut 137
  dovetail 137
  jig 137
  rip 137
  saber 137
  tenon 137
Scandinavian furniture 12,
  27, *27*, 68, 106, 110, *121*
scoops, wooden 25, 90, *90*,
  92
flour **92–3**
scrapers, cabinet 138
screwdrivers 139
screws 141, *141*
  countersinking 139, 141
  using 139, 141
settle-beds 19
settles 18
  "bacon" *18*, 19
  box 18
settle-tables 19

Shakers, the 12, 116
  boxes 84
  candle stands 34
  chairs 49, 65, 80
  hanging shelves 109, 116,
    116, **118–19**
  tables 78
sharpening tools 140
shelves, hanging *106*, 109,
  116, *116*, **118–19**
Shenandoah Valley, Va:
  furniture *16*
sideboards 80, 99
sleigh beds 106
"smallware" 83
smoothing planes 138
sofa, Chippendale-style *16*
spokeshaves 138
spoon racks 87, *87*, **88–9**
spoons, wooden 83, *84*, 87,
  87, **88**, 89, *90*
  love 87
staining wood 146
"stick-ups" (decoys) *31*
stools *18*, 27, 55, *55*, *78*
  "extended" 55
  milking 27, *27*, **28–9**
storage *see* boxes;
  chests-of-drawers;
  cupboards; peg-boards;
  settles; shelves *etc.*
stoves:
  portable 77
  woodburning *18*
Swedish furniture 27, *121*

T

tables 65
  bedroom 109, *109*
  dressing 109
  gate-leg 78
  kitchen/dining 39, 77–8
  Pembroke 78
  sawbuck 78
  settle 19
  Shenandoah Valley (pine)
    16
  side 39, *39*, **40–2**, 80
  tavern 80, *80*
  "ten-dollar" 78
  trestle 39, 77, 78
  "X"-frame 78
tallboys 109
tavern tables 80, *80*
tenon and socket joints 145
tenons *see* mortise and
  tenon joints; tenon
  and socket joints

tenon saws 137
testers 129
textiles, woven and quilted
  16, *16*
Thompson, Flora: *Lark Rise
  to Candleford* 16
Thonet bentwood furniture
  65
throws 16
tobacco boxes 22
tools, basic 134, 136–40
  sharpening 140
  see also power tools
towel rails, wooden 115
toy boxes 113
toys, wooden 113, *113*
trestle tables 39, 77, 78
trundle beds
  see beds, trundle
trunks 124, *124*
tubs, wooden 83, 84
twca cam (carving tool) 89
twist bits 139

U

utensils, kitchen
  see kitchens, utensils

V

varnishes 146
  "crackle" 147
verandahs 46, *46*, 49, *50*
  chairs for *49*, 65, **66–7**, 68,
    68, **70–1**
vises 136

W

wall paneling
  see paneling, wood
wallpapers 16
washstands, wooden 109
wax finishes 146, 147
  "antique" 147
weather vanes 58
Welsh dressers 83
whetting tools 140
whirligigs 58, *58*
  "Jack Chopping Wood"
    62, **60–2**
Windsor chairs *18*, *31*, 49,
  80, *96*
workbenches 136

X

"X"-frame tables 78

Y

Young, James 34

ACKNOWLEDGMENTS

I thank Judith More for asking me to write this book and for her support throughout, Sophie Pearse who was in at its birth, and Jenny Jones who saw it through its final, sometimes fraught, stages. Thanks to the Art Department and Production, and those background sub-editors, readers and illustrators who, bit by bit, helped us to put it all together. Thanks also to the Accounts Department, whose literary contribution – writing advance cheques – should not be overlooked.

Thanks to James Merrell for his superb photography; my American friends Merryll and Ed Saylan, who read part of the manuscript; Chris Mowe and Henryk Terpilowski for advice and help with the antique finishing; and Linda Fielder for word processing, again.

Finally, I would like to thank all those who, over the years, have taught me to love and understand wood and how to make useful things with it. And I thank God for the trees we all use.

The publishers would like to thank the following for kindly allowing us to photograph their homes:
Shirley Dupree, Jack Hill, Howard Kaplan, Tasha and Jack Polizzi, George Schmidt, Maryanne Wilkins

Antique and modern country-style furniture similar to that seen in the photographs can be obtained at:
T.P. Saddle Blanket & Trading 304 Main Street, Great Barrington MA, USA
Howard Kaplan Antiques 827 Broadway, New York NY 10003, USA
Howard Kaplan Bath 47 East 12th Street, New York NY 10003, USA
Makers 1 Ives Street, off Draycott Avenue, London SW3 2ND, England